First Edition

CW01572552

THE
CULTURAL ASPECT
OF THE
RISING SUN EMPIRE

Japan Viewed from Within

PAUL A. ETOGA

TABLE OF CONTENTS

PERSPECTIVE

Japan was once a mysterious and a remote country, but now, the Rising Sun Empire has become a multicultural society. Foreigners, like myself, have embraced Japanese culture through "manga", food, sport, education and other cultural elements that have attracted many of us attention and enriched our lives.

I am a Paris University graduate. Our university had a kind of exchange program with Keio University that allowed students to travel and spend some time with students of either campuses. I am one of those students who profited from such program in the summer of 1993. I was able come to Keio University new campus in Fujisawa, outside Tokyo.

That experience opened entirely my eyes. For example, I joined the Keio University soccer team and went to a "gasshuku" translated training camp, in Yamanaka ko not far from Mount Fuji. At the end of that training camp, many of my new friends then and I started to roam through Japan. We traveled to the Kansai region with a plan to visit as many temples as we could. Just to name a few, we visited the KINKAKUJI, the KOYOMIZU-DERA, the TODAIJI, the SANJUSANGEN-do and the GINKAKUJI etc. I remember that at night we would eat OKONOMIYAKI or RAMEN and other traditional Japanese sweeties. Then we traveled to Iwaki, a city located in Fukushima Prefecture, to visit the HAWAIIAN JOUBAN ONSEN (hot spring) and many more ONSEN after that. We also went to Kamakura, a city outside Tokyo. I was delighted to ride the Chinchin train there. After that experience, I had a story to tell to my classmates back to Europe. A story that was completely different from any story I had lived ever since I was born. Not to forget that I had experienced my first ever earth quake and the typhoon number 13, in September of that year.

Europeans, Americans and Africans as well have all embraced the Japanese culture. We love sushi because it is light and healthy food to eat.

From early age, French children, for instance, are captivated by the legend of Son Goku, a fictional character and main protagonist of the animated cartoon Dragon Ball series, created by Akira Toriyama. Son Goku messes up plans for evil to rule the world.

I am still one of adorable fans of Son Goku and his children Gohan and Goten. When I was in high school, I bought and collected Dragon Ball *manga* series just like many of my classmates back then. The amazing thing was that all those *manga* were written in Japanese language. And despite the fact that none of us could decipher the Japanese kanjis or kana, it did not matter much because we had to have them. Moreover, none of us would miss a single program of Dragon Ball on TV. The following day we would gather and discuss the episode we all watched the day before.

It is a fact that mass media and marketing have helped a lot in spreading Japanese culture throughout the world. Millions of derivative products are released every year then the snowball grows larger and larger and rolls on at full speed. One of the reasons Japanese culture has become so popular around the world is that Japanese language education has been integrated in schools programs in Europe and in America. Many schools do insert history, culture and political economy of Japan in their programs which makes it easy and convenient for students of the Japanese language to learn, understand and enjoy the Japanese culture.

According to the Japan foundation, there are now more and more learners of the Japanese language. As a matter of fact, institutions and teachers have increased tremendously in Europe and in the USA. The integration of the Japanese culture in western countries has made Japanese music performed by Baby Metal, a rock band of three young Japanese women, to be fully accepted despite the fact that they sing all their songs in Japanese.

By publishing this book, my intention is to continue telling the story of Japan and its culture the way I see it and the way I have lived it.

- Special thanks to Mama Junko and to Michiko sama for numerous photographs and explanations.

CHAPTER 1

PART 1

THE ORIGIN OF THE NAME JAPAN

Japanese people called their country Japan: ***Nihon*** or ***Nippon,*** written in KANJI 「日本」 meaning the " sun's origin" and translated in English the "***Land of the Rising Sun***" or in French "***le Pays du Soleil levan***t" This comes from the Chinese who referred to the Japan's eastern position relative to China.[1] Therefore, from China it appeared that the sun rose from the direction of Japan. Since Japan was an Empire then, it was called the "***Rising Sun Empire***" in English and "***L'Empire du Soleil Levant***" in French.

China has a great deal of influence on Japanese culture. It is said that the Japanese opted for the name Nihon for their country during the Sui Dynasty, because it was how the country was perceived from the Chinese perspective. The name, ***Nippon,*** was officially adopted in documents and manuscripts during the Taika reform in 645. However, before ***Nihon*** could be used officially, Japan was known as ***Wa*** or ***Wakoku***(倭国).[2] ***Wa*** was a name given by the Chinese who referred to an ethnic group who lived in Japan during the Three Kingdoms Period.[3]

---

[1] Nussbaum, Louis Frédéric et al. (2005). "*Nihon*" in Japan encyclopedia, p. 707.

[2] Joan, R. Piggott (1997). *The emergence of Japanese kingship.* Stanford University Press. pp. 143

[3] The Three Kingdoms was the tripartite division of China among the states of Wei, Shu and Wu (from 220 -280) Theobald (2000).

PART 2

JAPAN LANDSCAPE

Japan is a stratovolcano archipelago country of 6,852 islands[4] with a diversified landscape which is almost 70 percent mountainous. It stretches from north to south with many islands, mountains and valleys that split land unequally. The five main islands are **Hokkaido, Honshu, Shikoku, Kyushu** and **Okinawa**. Honshu is the largest of all and can be referred to as the mainland.

The relief

Japan is a part of the continent of Asia. The territory extends 377,975 km^2 in total (The land 364,485 km^2 and the water 13,430 km^2). [5] The topography of Japan shows an uneven country with rugged mountains, steep and deep valleys and plains. The alternation in sequence of mountains and valleys combined with a rocky soil leave Japan with less than 20 percent of arable land.

Japan has no land borders, the coastline measures 29,751 km. The highest point is Mount Fuji which rises up to 3,776 m and the lowest point is Hachiroogata with -4 m.

The longest and widest river in Japan is the Shinano River (Shinano gawa). It is 367 km long. It is located in the north east of Honshu. It flows through Nagano and Niigata prefectures before it reaches the Sea of Japan. The largest fresh water lake is Lake Biwa (Biwa-ko). It is located in the Shiga Prefecture, west-central of Honshu in the north of Kyoto.

---

[4] Defined as land more than 100 m in circumference.

[5] CIA WORLD FACTBOOK of September 2019

The climate

The climate of Japan varies from humid subtropical and tropical rainforest in the south (Okinawa Prefecture), to humid continental in the north (Hokkaido). Which means the south is warmer than the north.

Japan neighboring countries.

Japan does not have any international land borders. However, it shares maritime borders with the following countries: China, North Korea, South Korea, Russia, Taiwan and the Philippines.

Japan is separated from the People's Republic of China by the East China Sea. With North Korea, the Sea of Japan separates the two countries from the east coast of North Korea and South Korea is separated from Japan by the Korea Strait.

The maritime border between Russia and Japan is defined by several straits, including the La Perouse Strait, the Nemuro Strait, and the Sovietsky Strait. Taiwan and Japan are separated by the East China Sea and the Philippines are separated from Japan by the South China Sea.[6]

Chinese ideas and influences have helped shape Japanese culture more than any other country. For instance, Japan adopted the Chinese script for its own use and both Confucianism and Buddhism were imported into feudal Japan. Both countries signed a peace and friendship treaty in 1978 and ties between them have developed strongly ever since. At the same time the basic objective of Japan's foreign policy toward Asia has been to promote peace and prosperity, understanding and solidarity throughout the continent. Indeed, Japan has exercised its economic, political and

---

[6] World Atlas (world Facts)

diplomatic influence to support trends toward stability and discourage tendencies toward instability.[7]

Japan's view from space

Source: SeaWiFS Project, NASA/Goddard Space Flight Center, and ORBIMAGE - Cropped version of the high resolution variation of image found at:

http://visibleearth.nasa.gov/view_rec.php?id=1248,PublicDomain,

https://commons.wikimedia.org/w/index.php?curid=3454339

---

[7] 1978 Diplomatic Bluebook, published by the Ministry of Foreign Affairs. The edition covers the 1978 calendar year. The translation was prepared by the Foreign Press Center/Japan.

Japan and neighboring countries

Source: Map of Japan www.buzzle.com

CHAPTER 2

PART1

JAPAN NATIONAL ANTHEM AND MEANING "KIMIGAYO"

君が代は Kimigayo wa

千代に八千代に Chiyo ni yachiyo ni

さざれ石の Sazareishi no

巌となりて Iwao to narite

苔のむすまで Koke no musu made

English Translation:

May the reign of the Emperor

continue for a thousand, nay, eight thousand generations

and for the eternity that it takes

for small pebbles to grow into a great rock

and become covered with moss.

Kimigayo is the national anthem of Japan. Its lyrics are from a *waka* poem written in the Heian period (794-1185)[1] by an unknown author. The current melody was chosen in 1880, replacing the one composed by John William Feton a few years earlier.

---

[1] Japan – Kimigayo". National Anthems. Archived from the original on 2011-12-27 and retrieved 2011-11 28 by Wikipedia.

The title "Kimigayo" translated "His imperial Majesty's Reign" has no official translation or lyrics established in law.[2] "Kimigayo" has served as the national anthem of the Empire of Japan from 1888 to 1945. However, after World War II in1945, despite the fact that Japan surrendered and the Empire was dissolved, Emperor Hirohito was not dethroned and "Kimigayo" was retained as the national anthem. A parliamentary democracy was established therefore replacing a political system based on imperial sovereignty to one based on popular sovereignty.

Japan flag and meaning

Japan national flag is called *Nisshōki* (日章旗, the "flag of sun"), however, it is more commonly known as *Hinomaru* (日の丸, the "circle of the sun"). Japan national flag is a rectangular white banner bearing crimson-red dick at its center. This flag was designated as the national flag in the act on National Flag and Anthem, which was promulgated and became effective on August 13, 1999.

In Japan mythology and religion, the sun plays a very important role in which the Emperor is in the middle. The Emperor is said to be the direct descendant of the sun goddess *Amaterasu,* who founded the country Japan some 2,700 years ago. Therefore, the Emperor is the "son of the sun". The name of the country, the "Land of the Rising Sun" as well as the design of the flag reflect this central importance of the sun. The ancient history *Shoku Nihongi* (続日本紀) [3]says that Japan's flag was first used by *Emperor Monmu,* who used it representing the sun in court in 701. After

---

[2] <u>Source</u>: "Elementary schools face new mandate: Patriotism, 'Kimigayo'". The Japan Times Online. Kyodo News. 2008-03-29..

[3] Bender, Ross (March 2009), "Performative Loci of Shoku Nihongi Edicts, 749–770", Journal of Oral Tradition, 24 (1), pp. 249–268

that, the shoguns are also said to have used a sun flag in the 13th century when fighting against the Mongolian invasion.

Japan has various flags: the Japanese maritime forces flag, Japanese self-defense army forces flag, and Japanese emperor family flag etc.

Japan flags

National flag, adopted in 1870

War flag of the Imperial Army 1868-1945

Flag of the Imperial Navy 1889-1945

Self Defense Forces, in use since 1945

Maritime Self Defense Forces, in use since 1945

Standard of the Emperor, adopted in 1889

Source: www. Quora.com

PART 2
THE SYMBOLS OF JAPAN

National symbols of Japan are the symbols or icons that are used in Japan to represent what is unique. Any designated symbol reflects an aspect of Japan's culture and history.

Here are few symbols and their meaning.

This T-shape represents the post office and the zip code as well.

The zen circle: "***Enso***" means emptiness and the universe. People must empty their minds in order to understand the universe.[4]

Salt: Sumo wrestlers throw salt before a fight to purify the ring.[5]

Restaurants owners in Japan always place salt at the entrance to protect their business and themselves from evil spirits.

---

[4] <u>Source</u>: Mai-ko.com

[5] <u>Source</u>: idrottsforum.org

This statue is called "***Jizo***"or "ojizo-san" or "ojizo-sama". In Buddhism, it protects children and travelers. Red is a color of purification and it is used to keep the devil away. ***Jizo*** with red bib is said to protect kids' spirit, when they passed away before their parents.[6]

A Red or Orange gate is called ***"tori"***. It separates real life from spiritual life. One should not walk in the middle as the middle way is supposed to be used by the gods only.[7]

---

[6] Source: Mai-ko.com

[7] Source:Thestylescribe.com (Fushimi Inari in Kyoto, the ORANGE SHRINE)

Flying fish is called "***Koi-nobor***i" It is used to celebrate boys' day on May 5[th8]

In Japan, ***Cranes*** are symbols of longevity and good fortune. They are monogamous that is why they are used in weddings / The Paper crane is a symbol of peace.[9]

---

[8] Source: tiptoeingworld.com. Celebrating boys' day in Tokyo

[9] Source: Commons.wikipedia.org. (File Japanese kraanvogels in Akan International Crane center. Feb 2012

Deer are said to be messengers of God in Japan and should not be hunted. That is why they are in such great number in Nara.[10]

Lucky Daruma Doll, represents Bodidaruma who is the founder of zen in Buddhism. How do you use it? You paint the right eye before making a wish. When your wish has come true, you paint the left eye. It is said to bring luck.[11]

---

[10] Source: Soranews24.com. Shikadamari: The Nara deer summer gathering phenomenon that baffles visitors every year.

[11] Source: www.pinterest.com.au

CHAPTER 3

PART1

TOKYO, THE CAPITAL OF JAPAN AND A COSMOPOLITAN CITY

Tokyo was originally known as Edo (江戸), which means "estuary". It is a reference to the Sumida River and Tokyo Bay. The city of Edo started to develop after Tokugawa Ieyasu, a Japanese warrior founded the Tokugawa shogunate there in 1603.[1]

Tokugawa Ieyasu was originally named Matsudaira Takechiyo (松平竹千代), he was the son of Matsudaira Hirotada (松平広忠, 1526–1549), the lord of Mikawa, and O-Dai-no-kata (於大の方), the daughter of a neighboring samurai lord, Mizuno Tadamasa.[2]

Edo became a big city, by the mid-eighteen century it had a population of over one million people. Meanwhile, the Emperor resided in Kyoto, which was the capital back then. The Edo Period lasted for nearly 260 years until the Meiji Restoration in 1868. Meiji means "enlightenment".[3] That same year, the Tokugawa Shogunate ended and the imperial rule was restored. The Emperor moved to Edo, which was renamed Tokyo. That is how Tokyo became the capital of Japan.

Tokyo was administrated under two systems of government, Tokyo-fu (the prefecture) and Tokyo-shi (the city). However, in 1941, the Pacific War broke out and Tokyo was heavily affected. In order to assure great

---

[1] Source: Tokyo Metropolitan Government

[2] Source: BBC, Tokugawa Ieyasu's history (1542-1616)

[3] Source: Lonely planet "The Eastern Capital is born"

effectiveness in times of war, the two systems merged to become the Metropolis of Tokyo in 1943 and a governor was appointed.

When the war ended on the 2nd of September 1945, the government and the military surrendered. However, Tokyo had sustained great damage because of bombing and had paid a heavy cost in terms of population lost. As a matter of fact, Tokyo had lost nearly half of its 6 million people it had before the war started.

In May 1947 the new Constitution of Japan and the Local Autonomy Law took effect, and Seiichiro Yasui was elected the first Governor of Tokyo by popular vote under the new system.[4]

PART 2
THE DIVISION OF TOKYO

Tokyo is both a Metropolis and a Megalopolis.

Tokyo Metropolis is bordered to the east by the Edogawa River and Chiba Prefecture, to the west by mountains and Yamanashi Prefecture, to the south by the Tamagawa River and Kanagawa Prefecture, and to the north by Saitama Prefecture.

The Tokyo Megalopolis Region is made up of Tokyo and the seven surrounding prefectures including Saitama, Chiba, Kanagawa, Ibaraki, Tochigi, Gunma, and Yamanashi.

Tokyo Metropolis is a metropolitan prefecture with administrative entities of 23 special wards and municipalities. The 23 special wards (ku in

---

4 Tokyo Metropolitan Government (東京都年表)

Japanese) are in the center. The Tama area is made up of 26 cities (shi), 5 towns (machi), and 8 villages (mura) [5].

The 23 special wards of Tokyo

Source: www.123rf.com "Tokyo administrative map"

The demography of Tokyo

According to the UN World Urbanization Prospects, in 1950 the population of Tokyo was 11,274,641. Now in 2020, it is estimated at 37,393,129. Which means Tokyo has grown by 137,020 since 2015. It

---

[5] Tokyo Metropolitan Government "Tokyo's history, Geography and population"

represents a 0.07% annual change. These estimates represent the urban agglomeration of Tokyo, which includes suburban areas.

The population of Tokyo is very much diversified. Apart from the Japanese, there is a large number of foreigners who live in Tokyo. The largest ethnic group is the Chinese, followed by the Korean, the Philippines and Americans.

Eddokko (江戸っ子)

I am Eddokko. Are you? The Japanese dictionary defines as "Eddokko" a person who was born and raised in Edo/Tokyo. However, if one parent was not born and raised in Edo/Tokyo, then the child would not be a true Edokko and would be called *madara.(mottled).*[6]

The term is said to have taken root in the late 18th century in Edo. Being an Edokko also implied that the person had certain personality traits different from the non-native population, such as being assertive, straightforward, cheerful and proud.

Historically, Edokko exclusively refers to *Chōnin*,[7] the commoners. The majority of samurai in Edo were from the countryside, and Edokko enjoyed themselves by looking down on them, referring to them as being yabo, (unaesthetic, unappealing) the opposite of iki. About half of the Edo population was such samurai.[8]

---

[6] Chōnin (町人, "townsman") was a social class that emerged in Japan during the early years of the *Tokugawa* period. In the social hierarchy, it was considered subordinate to the warrior class.

[7] <u>Source</u>: Nishiyama, Matsunosuke (1997). Edo Culture: Daily Life and Diversions in Urban Japan, 1600-1868. Honolulu: University of Hawai'i Press. p. 204

[8] <u>Source</u>: Wikipedia, the free encyclopedia

The Governance of Tokyo

The Tokyo Metropolitan Government (東京都庁, Tōkyōto-chō) is the government of the Tokyo Metropolis. The government consists of a popularly elected governor and assembly. The headquarters building is located in the ward of Shinjuku. The metropolitan government administers the special wards, cities, towns and villages that constitute part of the Tokyo Metropolis.

The people of Tokyo directly elect the governor to four-year terms of office. There is no limit to the number of terms a person may serve. The current Governor is Yuriko Koike. She has been in office since 2016.

The people of Tokyo have been electing their governor since 1947, before that the governor was appointed.

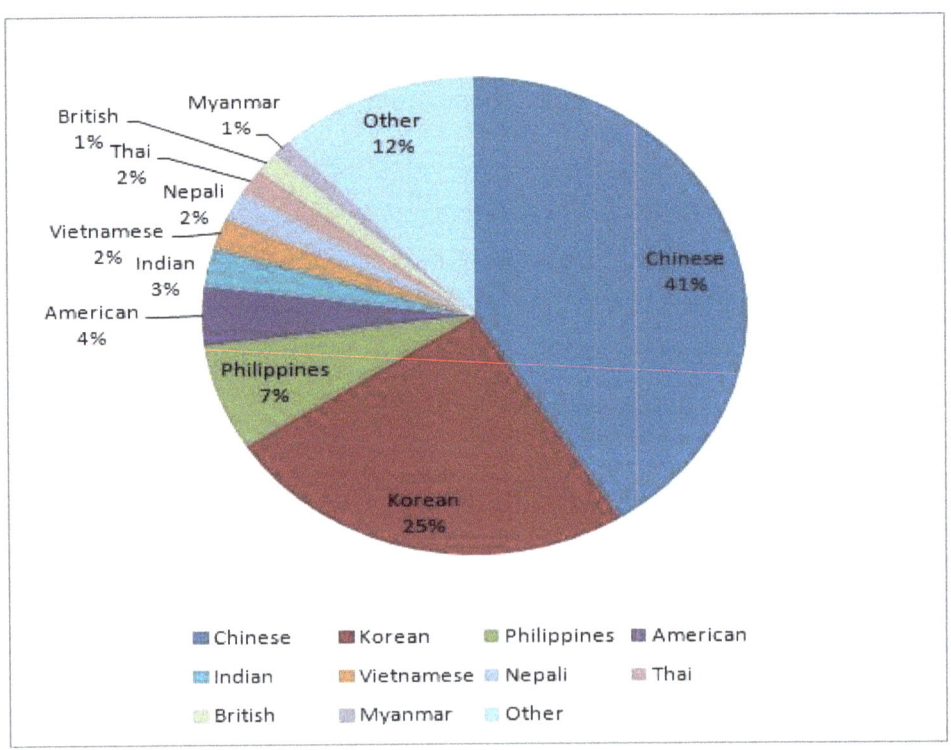

Source: Tokyo Metropolitan Government. (Foreigners in Tokyo)

CHAPTER 4

PART1

THE PEOPLE OF JAPAN

The natives of Japan archipelago are Japanese. It may not be obvious when you visit Japan for the first time, but Japanese are composed of different ethnic groups: The *Yamato*, the *Ryukyuan* the *Ainu*, and the *Burakumin.*

The Yamato (大和) are the largest ethnic group and count for 98% of the people of Japan [1]. The term Yamato referred to people of mainland Japan who were to be distinguished from other ethnic groups who were being incorporated into the Empire in the 1800s.

The Ryukyuan Japanese are indigenous from the Ryukyu Islands that extend up to Taiwan. The Ryukyu Japanese are themselves divided into subgroups (*Okinawan, Amami, Miyako, Yaeyama, Yonaguni people*) and speak one of the two main branches of the Japonic language [2].

The Ainu are a group of indigenous Japanese people concentrated on the Japanese island of Hokkaido, Kuril Islands, and the Russian island of Sakhalin.

The Burakumin are "hamlet people" or "village people". It referred to the segregated communities made up of laborers working occupations that

---

[1] World Atlas

[2] Masami Ito (12 May 2009). "Between a rock and a hard place". The Japan Times

were considered impure of tainted by death, such as executioners, butchers and undertakers.[3]

According to the Independent administrative agency of statistics center, the population of Japan is about 126.5 million. Within which Japanese count for 97.8% of the population. The remaining 2.2% of the total legal resident population are foreigners.

The Chinese are the largest foreign ethnic group with 0.64% of the population followed by the Korean at 0.40%.[4]

Samurai

The Samurai or (bushi), whose main weapon was the sword, were warriors who made up the ruling military class that became the highest ranking casted during the Edo Period (1603-1867). They had an ethic code called "bushido" which means "the way of the warrior".[5]

A samurai is characterized by his loyalty to his master, ethical behavior, self-discipline and respectful. It is what Japanese are known for around the world.

PART 2
THE JAPANESE LANGUAGE

Japanese (日本語, Nihongo) is the main and the official language spoken in Japan. Outside Japan, there is a large number of Japanese descendants who speak Japanese in Hawaii and in Brazil.

---

[3] BBC, Mike Sunda: specialist in music and Japanese youth and urban culture

[4] Independent administrative agency of statistics center (独立行政法人統計センター)

[5] Japan-guide.com

The origin of the Japanese language is unclear. However, some link it to the Altaic language family, which includes **Turkish, Mongolian, Manchu** and **Korean.** The Japanese language also shows similarities to **Austronesian languages like Polynesian.**[6] Some similarities of Japanese can also be found in **EWONDO**, a local language spoken in Yaoundé, the capital of Cameroon in West Africa. Example: **Ewondo** uses the word **bichobicho**（びちょびちょ）with the same pronunciation and exactly the same meaning "**wet**" as in Japanese. To be further investigated…

The Characteristics of the Japanese language

Writing

The Japanese writing system consists of three different character sets: the Kanjis (漢字：Chinese characters) and the Kana composed of Hiragana（かんじ＝**kanji**）and Katakana（カンジ＝Kanji）(two syllabaries of 46 characters each). Japanese texts can be written in two ways: In Western style, in horizontal rows from the top to the bottom of the page, or in traditional Japanese style, in vertical columns from the right to the left side of the page. Both writing styles are still being used today.

Grammar

Basic Japanese grammar is relatively simple. But there are complicated factors such as gender articles and distinctions between plural and singular that are difficult to detect in a sentence. Sometimes they are completely missing. Conjugation rules for verbs and adjectives are simple and almost do not have exceptions. Nouns are not declinated, but appear always in the same form.

---

[6] Independent administrative agency of statistics center (独立行政法人統計センター)

Pronunciation

When compared with other languages, the Japanese language has relatively few sounds. It may be the easiest language in terms of pronunciation. Personally speaking, when I started learning Japanese, I found it very easy at the beginning although things got a bit complicated later on. The biggest difficulties are accents, which do exist, but to a much lower degree than in the Chinese language. Moreover, there are many homonyms in words that are pronounced the same way, but have different meanings.

Speech

Unlike most western languages, Japanese use different expressions when talking to an unknown person or a superior, as opposed to when talking to a child, family member or a close friend. There is an extensive grammatical system to express politeness and formality. Broadly speaking, there are three levels of speech in spoken Japanese: the plain form **"kudaketa Nihongo"** (くだけた 日本語= casual or informal language), the simple polite form **"teineigo"** (丁寧語= polite or formal language) and the advanced polite form **"keigo"** (敬語 = honorific language).

Since most relationships are not equal in Japanese society, one person typically may have a higher position. This position is determined by a variety of factors including job, age or experience. The person in the lower position is expected to use a polite form of speech, whereas the other might use a plainer form.

Dialects in Japan

It is not always obvious, but Japan counts many dialects called:

-   **"hoogen"** (方言) or **"ben"**(弁) such as Hokkaido-ben, sendai-ben, Osaka-ben, Kyoto-ben, Hiroshima-ben, Fukuoka-ben etc…

-   or sometimes called **"kotoba"**(言葉). Example: Edo-kotoba which means **Edo language**.

- or "**namari**" (訛り). Example: Toohoku-namari, meaning Toohoku accent.

All these languages are not taught in classrooms but they are still spoken although in decline. They all differ from "**Hyoojungo**" (標準語 = standard) or "**kyootsuugo**" (共通語) meaning common language spoken in Tokyo, which has spread through the country thanks to modernization. [7]

---

[7] hougen.u-big.org

CHAPTER 5

PART 1

EDUCATION IN JAPAN

The academic year in Japan starts from April and ends in March of the following year, with summer vacation from August to mid-September. Winter vacation is from the end of December to the beginning of January and spring break from the end of March to the beginning of April. There are five cycles in Japanese education. Every cycle starts with "**nyugakushiki**" (入学式 = entrance ceremony) and ends with "**sotsugyoushiki**" (卒業式 = graduation ceremony).

The five cycles of Japanese education

In Japan, school is divided into five cycles:

- " **Yōchien**" (幼稚園=Nursery school) age:3~6

- " **Shōgakkō**" (小学校= Elementary school) age: 6~12

- " **Chūgakkō**" (中学校 = Middle school) age: 12~15

- " **Kōkō**" (高校 = High school) age: 15~18

- "**Daigaku**" (大学 = University) or " **Senmongakkō**" (専門学校 = Vocational school) age: from 18 and above.

School is compulsory from Nursery to Middle school, which means from 3 to 15 years old. In japan, almost every middle school graduate enrolls in high school. Students enrolled in public schools until Middle school do not pay registration or school material fees. Families pay secondary costs such as meals and school trips.

PART 2

SCHOOL UNIFORM

Japan introduced school uniforms "*seifuku*" (制服) in the late 19th century [1]. Now days, school uniforms are almost universal in public and private schools system. A uniform is also required in some women's colleges.

All elementary schools do not require students to wear a uniform. But when a uniform is compulsory, boys wear white shirts, shorts and caps. Girls' uniforms can include a grey or green pleated skirt and a white blouse or the sailor outfit. Boys and girls often wear brightly colored caps, like yellow visible enough from a certain distance to prevent traffic accidents.

Junior and senior-high-school students also wear uniforms. Boys wear a white shirt, a tie, a blazer or a sweater vest with the school badge "*Kōshō*" (校章), tailored trousers and brown or black penny loafer shoes. Girls wear skirts even in winter.

Source: Seifuku-ichiba.com/ kaetsu women's High School

---

[1] K12 academics: School Uniforms in Japan

<u>Source</u>: Seifuku-ichba.com/ kaetsu ariake Junior & High School uniform for girls.

PART 3

SCHOOL LIFE ORGANIZATION

Students in Japan are very busy. Classes are held from Monday to Friday and half days every two Saturdays. After classes some students would attend "*juku*" (塾 = cram school) in order to prepare for entrance exams or raise their general level of education in some targeted subjects like mathematics or English. Students who have voluntarily registered in clubs such as basketball, soccer, volley, kendo, just to name a few, would join their practice session.

Up to high school, Japanese students are educated in a way that they themselves are responsible for keeping their classes or their school clean. Students are often divided into small groups from which some swipe the board, some sweep the floor and some mop it. A lot of people may find it excessive, but in the end, it helps build bond between students and it teaches them how to work as a team in order to achieve goals.

Then every year, every school has to organize their school festival which is very demanding. The festival is a display of activities such as sport competitions, cultural exhibitions, plays, songs performed by the students' band etc… It usually takes more than half a year to prepare for that big event that takes place on Saturday and Sunday between September and November.[2] The following Monday all participants must come and clean up the mess. Then on Tuesday, all regular classes resume. At the end of the day, students are very exhausted.

PART 4
ENTRANCE EXAMINATIONS

Every student has to take an entrance exam in order to move up to junior high school, high school, or university. Those exams are generally quite difficult and require long hours of studies. Thus, for a better test preparation, many students need assistance. That is the main reason students attend cram schools after regular classes, particularly if they target one specific school or university.

---

[2] The preparations are done by students on their own time after classes and during the summer vacations. Sometimes they are assisted by a teacher or professor who acts as the "***kurabu komon***" (クラブ顧問=club adviser)

CHAPTER 6

PART 1
RELIGION BELIEFS IN JAPAN

There are Catholic churches, Christian chapels as well as other religion worship places in Japan but Shinto and Buddhism are the main religions. In ancient times, the Japanese believed that all natural phenomena such as animals and plants etc... possessed **kami** "神"meaning divine power or God. This belief came to be known as Shinto and was established as an official religion. Buddhism instead was imported from the mainland in the 6th century. Ever since, the two religions have co-existed harmoniously.[1]

Religion is a private matter in Japan. Japanese do not discuss religion in public and do not worship regularly. Having said that, I have attended Matsubara Kyoukai （松原教会）located in Setagaya and Kichijouji Catholic Church located in Kichijouji (カトリック吉祥寺教会= Kichijouji Catholic Church), both churches are in Tokyo and they were always full on Sundays. Each time, two third of the worshipers were Japanese. This may prove that many Japanese are now worshiping more than they used to.

All year long, Japanese people participate in birth, marriage and death rituals, as well as in spiritual festivals (祭=**matsuri**). Which can be interpreted as worshiping, as a monk is always involved. A monk would be the equivalent of a priest or a pastor in Western countries. Moreover, almost all Japanese observe customs that have origins in Buddhism or Shintoism, but yet many still define themselves as atheists. It leaves you

---

[1] https://culturalatlas.sbs.com.au/japanese-culture

scratching your head, when you look at the amount of work done preceding some of these events.

You wonder why someone would go through such pain to prepare for a huge Buddhist or Shinto connoted festival or any other ceremony, which is also time consuming, if he or she did not believe in the philosophy behind that particular event in the first place.

PART 2
SHINTOISM VERSUS BUDDHISM

- Shinto

Shinto is said to be an indigenous religion of Japan. It has no founder or sacred scripture but has been rooted in Japanese belief and traditions since the origins of Japan. Its philosophy is grounded in the value of man's relationship to nature. The main belief of Shinto is that everything that exist such as an animal, a tree, a flower, or water has a spirit, therefore it is '*kami*', or god. Thus, when treated with respect these kami can intervene somewhat and bring positive benefits into people's lives. Which means when someone goes to a shrine it is to worship one specific *kami.*

The diversity of religions in Japan now days shows that not all Japanese believe in the mythology and philosophy of Shinto. However, the majority people still take part in Shinto's practices as part of social and cultural tradition rather than a religion, because that heritage obviously needs to be preserved. At the same time, Shintoism seems to coexist with Buddhism or Catholicism and other religions that have multiplied in Japan.

- Buddhism

Buddhism is a philosophy built around the belief that people can reach a state of enlightenment in which they obtain the love, wisdom and clarity to see reality clearly and exist in it purely.[2]

Buddhism teaching is based on "The Four Noble Truths". They are as follow: firstly, there is suffering; secondly, that suffering has a cause; third, suffering has an end; and finally, there is a path to the end of suffering (The Eightfold Path) [3]. Therefore, a Buddhist must follow a path towards leading a moral life. If you seek to develop wisdom and understanding, you must be mindful of your thoughts and actions.

This can be achieved by practicing methods such as meditation in order to gradually overcome negative mindsets. Buddhism views human life as a continual repetitive cycle of birth and death as it is being move towards enlightenment.

Zen, which is very well known through the world as "Zen Buddhism", is only part of Buddhism. It emphasizes a close connection to nature and the role of a teacher as opposed to deities in guiding one towards spiritual knowing. Zen teachings value the stimulation of one's intuition through poems, conundrums and exercising expressive thinking through painting.

PART 3
RELIGIOUS CEREMONIES

All events religious or not to be commemorated and observed are marked in red in the Japanese calendar. Among those events, the New Year is certainly the most important time of the year observed from the 1st to the 3rd of January, followed by O-Bon, also observed on the 16th of August.

---

[2] https://culturalatlas.sbs.com.au/japanese-culture

[3] https://culturalatlas.sbs.com.au/japanese-culture

During the New Year celebration, most Japanese would make trips to their ancestral graves to pray for their late relatives. They would also visit the shrine to pray in order to secure luck for the upcoming year.

At O-Bon, it is believed that the spirits of the ancestors come down to earth to visit the living. These spirits are welcomed, which is an opportunity for the Japanese to visit their family graves.

Japanese families also celebrate the births of their children by visiting shrines. The childhood is commemorated at three key ages: three, five and seven. Each time, small children are dressed in kimonos and taken to the shrine.

Adulthood is officially celebrated at age 20 in Japan. Ceremonies are held in town halls followed by the visit to the shrine by young people dressed in kimonos.

Most Japanese weddings celebration can be in several parts. It can include a Shinto ceremony in traditional dress at a shrine and a Western-style wedding in a chapel as well, follow by a reception in a hotel or restaurant. In the second part, a bride can wear a wedding gown.

Japanese are anecdotally said to *"**be born Shinto, live a nonreligious life, wed Christian and die Buddhist"*** I wonder why?

Funerals are always overseen by Buddhist monk. Most Japanese dead are cremated and their ashes buried under the family gravestone.

The majority of Japanese festivals *"**matsuri"*** are connected to shrines. The traditional "matsuri" parades and rituals relate the cultivation of rice and the spiritual wellbeing of the local community.

CHAPTER 7

PART1
TRADITION AND CUSTOMS

Japanese people have been able to preserve their traditions and customs ever since Japan was created. When you visit Japan, even for a few days, it is very easy to notice and appreciate the uniqueness of lifestyle of the Japanese people. You will see people bowing to greet one another. You will hear a lot of the word "irashaimase" (いらっしゃいませ), which means welcome. The store or restaurant staff will say this every time a person comes in and it is the norm in Japan.

Japan has a unique culture with a very strict code of etiquette. For instance:

There would be specific toilet slippers kept inside the toilets, so you will have to take off your house slippers and put on the toilet slippers. Then, when entering a Japanese home, a traditional restaurant, temples or an art gallery, any time you come across of row of slippers, you should put them on.

There is also a specific away to accept gifts in Japan, otherwise you might inadvertently insult your host. This complex web of social rules and traditions can be overwhelming for whoever visit Japan for the first time, but you come to understand that, that is how it works in Japan. You get used to this new way of living relatively fast, from there on you start to appreciate what Japan society is made of.

PART 2

MATCHA CEREMONY

Tea ceremony or Matcha (抹茶) or "sadou" （茶道＝ translated "the way of tea"） or "chadou" is an aesthetically amazing experience. It is one of these Japanese beautiful customs to watch and to be part of. It is the kind that allows you to experience the Japanese food culture.

A lady would be dressed in a kimono in order to serve matcha with hot water boiled in an old-fashioned kettle, she stirs it up with a little wooden whisk. Every movement looks simple but coordinated. As the hostess's hands are considered part of the ceremony, it makes you forget for a while the reason why you came there in the first place. When the final product comes, it is green, thick and bitter tea that you are served with.

Learning how to serve matcha is a process that requires patience and concentration

The History of Sadou

The tradition of the Tea Ceremony dates back to the 9th century. The ***Nihon Koki(日本後紀)*[1]** a Japanese history text, relates of the Buddhist monk Eichu who, after returning from China, personally served sencha (unground green tea) to the emperor in the style of what then, over the span of roughly 700 years became known as sadou. Originating from China, the Japanese Tea Ceremony underwent evolution during the years, developing its own style, specifics, and rites.

The tea Ceremony environment

The environment plays a big role when performing sadou.

- The Tea Room(茶室 *cha-shitsu*): the ceremony cannot be performed anywhere. A Tatami room is necessary and the placement of the mats determines the position of host and guests.

- Dressing code: to honor the uniqueness of ceremony, the dress code is formal. The host will always wear a kimono, depending on what kind of ceremony is held. However, guests will be allowed to wear a suit or a kimono.

- Hanging Scroll: a hanging scroll can be found in the alcove called tokonoma. They usually display a painting or calligraphy, referring to the ceremony itself.

- Flower Vase: a small vase containing a flower arrangement, displayed in the tokonoma. Seasonal flowers are used alongside bamboo, rattan, or ceramics.

---

[1] Nihon Kōki (日本後紀) is an officially commissioned Japanese history text. Completed in 840, It covers the years 792–833

- The service is composed of "Matcha and Wagashi (和菓子=Japanese sweets). It is an afternoon tea time usually served with fresh, seasonal ingredients that stress the season the ceremony is held in.

- If you are the guest, bow and take the bowl with the right hand and place it on the palm of your left hand.

- Rotate the bowl three times clockwise with your right hand.

- Wipe the bowl where your lips touched it with the right hand, rotate it counter clockwise and return it to the host.

The philosophy behind Matcha or Sadou or Chadou

Matcha ceremony is not only about serving tea. It is a mental discipline to pursue the philosophy of wabi-sabi.[2] The utensils, like jugs, cups, and bowls, are intentionally kept simple with no decoration on them. They sometimes have an uneven shape or a little dent, which is done on purpose. That is to say: "beauty is found in imperfection. Accepting this fact, the participants honor imperfection by pouring their heart into the ceremony and having tea in a calm and relax state of mind.

Sadou is taught in many schools in Japan with an official instructor. Students who are interested often join the *sadou bu (茶道部 = Tea Ceremony Club)*.

---

[2] "Wabi-sabi is a world view centered on the acceptance of transience and imperfection. The aesthetic is sometimes described as one of beauty that is "imperfect, impermanent, and incomplete". Wikipedia

Source: www. Google. Co.jp /Hello Book Webshop/match utensils

Source: ja.wikipedia.org (matcha utensil)

Source://www.shoueido.jp/news/387 (Japanese sweets)

Source: www.toraya-group.co.jp (Japanese sweets)

<u>Source</u>: Japanese tea utensils - Wikipedia

<u>Source</u>: esterobayoliveoil.com/ Handcrafted Bamboo Matcha Set

PART 3

CHERRY BLOSSOM IN JAPAN

In Japan, the appearance of cherry blossoms, known as **sakura,** signals the beginning of "**Hanami**"(花見＝flower viewing). There are forecasts pinpointing exactly by the Japan Meteorological Corporation (JMC) when and where the flowers are expected to bloom, starting in March until early May. The milder the climate, the earlier the blossoms open, so the blossom-time can be observed from the south to the north of Japan

For example, in Okinawa, a subtropical island in southern of Japan, cherry blossoms open as early as January. While in Hokkaido, in the north, the flowering can be observed in May. In cities like Tokyo, Kyoto and Osaka, the cherry blossom season typically begins in early April.

The blooming time can be unpredictable sometimes, as the weather plays a very important role in it. If the weather during the months and weeks preceding the cherry blossom season is mild, blossoms will open early. If it is cold, blossoms will open later.

"Sakura" season is a big event that is celebrated and that attracts viewers from all over the world. That is why it is important to determine the blooming time of cherry trees and the geographical location.

For Japanese people thought, when the cherry get to "**mankai**"(満開＝full bloom), it means it is time for "**hanami**".

Hanami

The cherry blossom (sakura) has been celebrated in Japan for many centuries, I was once told, and holds a very particular place in Japanese culture. There may be many varieties of cherry tree in Japan, but most bloom for no longer than two weeks in spring. The Japanese celebrate this time of the year with **Hanami** (cherry blossom viewing) parties: friends, family or colleagues from work gather and picnic sitting on plastic mats under the blossoming trees. They drink, eat, sing and chat. Sometimes some people get higher than usual.

Tokyo: Kaetsu University Campus: The Sakura in full bloom

Tokyo: Kaetsu University Campus: The Sakura in full bloom

A few spot to join for Hanami

During the cherry blossom season, parks are open every day. Most are conveniently situated near a number of restaurants, entertainment, and various shops, which is ideal for people who would like to enjoy cherry blossom viewing and who wish to find an easily accessible location.

With millions of cherry trees of various kinds, including early and late blooming cherry blossoms, here are some of the best places to go for cherry blossom viewing in Tokyo.

- Shinjuku Gyoen National Garden, located some 10 minutes' walk away from Shinjuku station.

- Koishi Korakuen Garden, located 8 minutes' walk from Korakuen station.

- Ueno Park, located near Ueno station.

- Chidorigafuchi, located in the Hanzomon area.

- Inokashira Park, located in Kichijouji.

PART 4
ONSEN (温泉＝HOT SPRING), SENTŌ AND SUPER SENTŌ

Public bathing at the **onsen**, **sentō** or **super sentō**, is an old tradition in the Japanese culture, that is why they can be found almost everywhere in Japan. The presence of an onsen or sentō or super sentō somewhere is often indicated by the kanji: （湯＝yu） or hiragana （ゆ＝yu） meaning "hot water".

Onsen

The two kanji (温泉) read ***onsen*** literally mean "hot" and "source", which is the fundamental definition of a hot spring. However, in order to be officially recognized as an ***onsen*** in Japan, a hot spring must meet the following criteria:

1. The water must be at least 25°C (degrees Celsius) at the source.

2. One of 19 criteria, relating to the mineral content of the water, must be met. These are such as: metaboric acid (HBO2) greater than 5mg per 1kg, hydrogen ion greater than 1mg per 1kg, etc.[3]

Most ***onsen*** are built with ***roten buro*** (露天風呂) and ***noten buro*** (野天風呂) which means respectively outdoor and indoor bath.

The volcanic nature of Japan provides thousands of springs or ***onsen*** throughout the country. As a matter of fact, Japan is located along the Pacific Ring of Fire, which is said to be the most active earthquake belt in the world and volcanic eruptions regularly occur in that area. Within the Ring of Fire, several tectonic plates including: the Pacific Plate beneath the Pacific Ocean and the Philippine Sea Plate mash and collide.[4]

Onsen are known to have healing proprieties. When the ***onsen*** water contains distinctive minerals or chemicals, the ***onsen*** establishments typically display what type of water it is.[5]

Examples of types of onsen:

● Sulphur onsen (硫黄泉, iō-sen)

---

[3] www.Japanistry.com

[4] www.livescience.com/54434-why-so-many-earthquakes-strike-japan.html

[5] "Onsen (hot springs) in Japan—transforming terrain into healing landscapes".
https://doi.org/10.1016/j.healthplace.

- Sodium chloride onsen (ナトリウム泉, natoriumu-sen)

- Hydrogen carbonate onsen (炭酸泉, tansan-sen)

- Iron onsen (鉄泉, tetsu-sen)

- Ordinary onsen (単純泉, tanzyun-sen

Sentō

Sentō is also written with two kanji (銭湯) meaning: "coin" and "hot water". Sentōs are local establishments practical for people who do not have a bathtub or heated water at home. They may not be as luxurious and aesthetically pleasing as onsen, but they are still convenient for daily hygiene. Just by sitting in a large hot bath after a hardworking day can be relaxing, therefore it can be comfortable because it allows you to release stress to some degree. Some sentōs also add bath salts, herbs, wine etc. to the otherwise ordinary heated water in order to enhance health benefits.

A number of sentō have been closing down lately for various reasons. But a densely packed city like Tokyo, with smaller houses and apartments, needs local sentos for the benefit of families who cannot afford a bathtub or a trip to an onsen.

Super sentō

Super sentōs, commonly called (*suuppaa sentō*), are bathing houses as well. They are a bit more expensive than sentō and offer a wide variety of bathtubs, saunas, and other services such as massage, hairdressers, cafes, restaurants. Super sentōs cannot be technically called onsen because they do not use natural water, although they also have health benefits.

Tokyo, Mitaka: Chiyonoyu Sentō's founder himself on the signboard

Chiyonoyu Sentō's Entrance

Chiyonoyu sentō

Chiyonoyu Sentō's garden

CHAPTER 8

PART 1
GREETING IN JAPAN

Greetings, *aisatsu* (挨拶) are important in the Japanese culture, as it is in Cameroon, (Western Africa), China, France, Singapore, in the UK or in the US, countries that I have known well. However, the way the Japanese people greet one another is more than just "hi!" or "hello!" Throughout the day you will hear "*konnichiha*" (こんにちは)、 "*Konbanha*"(こんばんは) or "*irasshaimase*" (いらっしゃいませ) and so forth. Then you will see people bow and occasionally some will shake hands or even hug.

Why is there such disparity in greetings in Japan? It is because you have to follow a certain etiquette. Sometimes it is a matter of modesty or respect and sometimes it is just only the custom.

Bowing

In general, Japanese people greet one another by bowing. This form of greeting is called *ojigi* (お辞儀). In Japan, I have learnt that a bow could be formal or informal according to the situation. A formal bow can be graded as "**saikeirei**"(最敬礼=higher salute) or "**keirei**" (敬礼= salute) [1]

Saikeirei is a gesture performed as a way to express your sincere apology to someone or to express your profound gratitude. You will then bend over, lowering your torso and your head to an angle that is close to 45 degrees.

---

[1] Wikimedia Commons

Keirei bow is commonly performed in business relation. It is a sign of respect. Your will bend over your torso and your head to an angle close to 30 degrees.

Eshaku (会釈)　is an informal bow is performed among friends or colleagues. You bend over your torso and your head slightly to an angle that is close to 15 degrees.

Source: Wikimedia Commons. Formal bow

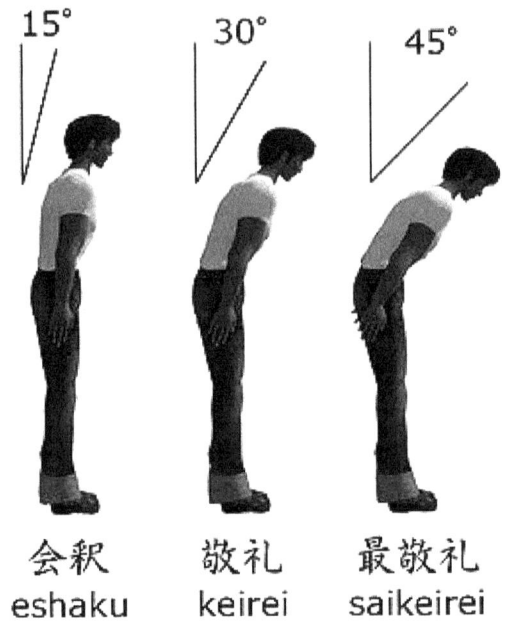

会釈
eshaku

敬礼
keirei

最敬礼
saikeirei

Source: www.en.Wikimedia.org: ojigi

PART 2

JAPANESE HONORIFIC ("SAN", "SAMA" "SHI" "TONO OR DONO" "KUN", "CHAN")

Japanese use various honorific in order to say **Miss, Mrs. Mr. Sir, and Madam**. In Japanese culture, it is important to know how to use them in everyday life. It is a mix of politeness and it indicates the type of relationship you have with other people.

The most important think to know is that Japanese people seldom call other people by their first name, therefore the honorific will be attached to the family name and will be placed after the name, unlike English or French for instance.

San (さん)

Example, to say Miss, Ms., Mrs. or Mr. Kobayashi, you would say Kobayashi **san.** This suffix is commonly used, regardless of the social status of a person and can even be used to a company or business names such as "yaoya san" (八百屋さん＝a greengrocer).

Sama (さま、様)

The suffix **Sama** is the most formal and it is a higher version of san. Sama will be used to indicate that the person has a high status. Ex: tennou sama (天皇様 ＝ Emperor) or Kami sama (神様＝ God).

Sama would also be used with customers: "kyaku sama" but the prefix "**o**" will be added and become "**okyakusama**" (お客様) it shows the degree of higher consideration toward the customer.

Shi (氏)

The suffix **Shi** is used in formal writing and sometimes in very formal speech, when a person is not familiar to the speaker. Ex: Tanaka shi (田中氏) "Shi" is often used in legal document at the city hall and newsreaders most of the time use "shi" to refer to people.

Dono/tono

Tono or dono (殿＝Lord or Master), is not commonly used in regular conversation. Tono or dono is often used in some types of written business correspondence, certificates and awards. It also indicates that the person referred to, has a high rank and commands respect from the speaker.

Kun (くん、君)

The suffix **Kun** seen as masculine, used for teenagers and young male. Kun is usually used by people seen as superior. This honorific will be mostly used when one person of higher status is talking to a younger person. Kun is beneath **san** and **sama**, with means the level politeness is very low.

Chan (ちゃん)

Chan is mostly used to refer to young children female you are familiar or have a close relationship with. Chan is said to have come from small children who could not say **san**. The use of **chan** toward an adult not familiar to you is considered to be condescending and offensive. But when used toward an adult who is very close to you, it is affectionate.

PART 3: IRASSHIAIMASE OR YOUKOSO

In Japanese culture, in stores and restaurants, customers are always greeted with enthusiasm. You would hear: "irasshiaimase (いらっしゃいませ= welcome), whenever you enter a shop or restaurant. This expression usually does not expect a response. It is also the first greeting you hear at the airport in Japan when coming from abroad.

Shitsurei shimasu

Shitsurei shimasu (失礼します) is one of these expressions you will hear throughout the day in Japan and that are difficult to explain to someone who is not familiar with the Japanese culture. When entering a room where there are already people who got there before you, you will have to say "Shitsurei shimasu" (失礼します= pardon me). And when you leave with people still in the room, you will have to say "shitsurei shimashita" (失礼しました= sorry for disturbing).

Then, when leaving your workplace before your colleagues, the Japanese will simply say: "Osaki ni shitsurei shimasu (お先に失礼します＝Sorry for leaving ahead of you) and your colleagues will reply: "otsukare sama deshita"(お疲れ様でした= Thank you for your hard work). As if someone else has to evaluate the amount of work you have completed on the day, which is not necessarily the case, although that may occur in some situations.

CHAPTER 9

PART 1

JAPANESE FAVORITE PASTIME: SPORT

In Japan, sport is divided into two categories: modern or imported sports that includes baseball, football known as soccer, basketball and tennis etc... And traditional sports or martial arts that includes kendo, karate, aikido and sumo etc... With such a variety of sports, which one to choose?

Sport in general plays an important role in Japanese culture. Starting from schools, Japanese children are encouraged to join sport clubs of their choice among the variety of sports offered, with a purpose above all to develop children physical ability, have them stayed active and healthy. Through sport clubs, children learn to develop a sense of belonging to a group and a sense of solidarity with other children. During the academic year, there are baseball, basketball and soccer competitions etc. organized among schools within which clubs from different schools take part. This helps to foster a sense of unity among children. Later on, some of these young men and women will continue to play as professionals in their favorite sport, and some will continue to enjoy their sports subjectively their entire life.

Japan can objectively be considered a sporting nation, in that there is a lot of interest in a variety of sports among Japanese. This is justified by the presence of many Japanese athletes in all major international sports event around the globe.

Soccer and baseball may be the most popular sports in Japan, because these two sports are the most widely watched. However, sport like golf, table tennis, tennis and swimming are not far behind.

The Ministry of Education, Culture, Sports, Science, and Technology known as ***Monbu-kagaku-shō*** (文部科学省), is responsible for sports management in Japan. The Japan Sports Agency actively promotes physical education and health, as well as maintaining the country's ability to compete in international athletics. So far, Japan has hosted major international sports even such as the Winter Olympics in 1972 and 2009, FIFA World Cup co-hosted with South Korea in 2002, the World Baseball Classic in 2006~2009 and the Rugby World Cup in 2019. Tokyo was set to host the 2020 Summer Olympics but because of the Covid-19 pandemic, the Games have been postponed to 2021.

Japan commemorates the Health and Sports Day every year, known as Sports Day ***Supōtsu no hi*** (スポーツの日). That day, formerly called "Physical education day" ***Taiiku no hi*** (体育の日), is a national holiday and observed. The Health and Sport Day was launched in 1966 to commemorate the 1964 Summer Olympics held in Tokyo and was celebrated the Second Monday of October,[1] but that date was moved to July 24 in 2020.

Sports Day, schools across Japan hold Track and Field events that begin early in the morning until late in the afternoon. These events are held in the spirit of the Olympics with a variety of sports events covered by local media.

PART 2
MARTIAL ARTS IN JAPAN.

The origin of traditional sports or martial arts or ***budō*** (武道=**way of war**) in Japan can be traced back to medieval times. During the Edo era (1603-1867)[2] people who belonged to the highest-ranking social were called

---

[1] www.Wikipedia.org

[2] Tokyo Metropolitan Government

Samurai or the **bushi** (武士) These warriors practiced and taught combat skills that restricted the use of weapons.

JŪDŌ or JUUDOO or JUUDOU

Jūdō（柔道）means "the gentle way". It is a martial art developed by Dr. Jigoro Kano in 1882 [3]. People who practice Jūdō are called **"Jūdōka"** (柔道家).   Jūdōkas use a series of techniques including ground techniques, choking and joint locking. Jūdō is a globally known sport that has become popular thank to its introduction in the Olympics in 1964 during the Tokyo Games[4]. Jūdōkas fight barefoot and their wear is called Jūdōgi (柔道着).

KARATE

Karate (空手) means "empty hand", from karate there is the word **"karatedo"** (空手道), meaning "the way of the empty hand". Karate is another martial art among traditional Japanese sport. It originated in Okinawa and has its origins in Chinese martial arts, in the Shaolin temple [5].

The modern karate known today is said to have been founded by Gichin Funakoshi (船越 義珍 Funakoshi Gichin, 1868–1957). It is characterized by linear punching and kicking techniques executed from a stable, fixed stance. Karate practitioners are called **"karateka"** (空手家)**. Karatekas** fight barefoot and hands. As a karateka, you have different levels to graduate from as you climb higher in the ranks.

Kendō or Kendou or Kendoo

Kendō (剣道), means "the way of the sword". It is said to be the oldest discipline of budo, Japanese martial arts. Kendō is a kind of fencing

---

[3] www.japan-experience.com

[4] www.joc.or.jp

[5] wikipedia.org / www.shaolin.org.cn

practiced with armor, **"bōgu"** (防具) or **kendōgu** (剣道具,)"kendō equipment", a wooden sword, **"bokken"or "bokutou"**(木剣, 木刀), and bamboo, **"shinai"** (竹刀). Kendō also has an important spiritual side, intended to strengthen determination. Practitioners of kendō are called kendōka (剣道家), meaning "someone who practices kendō"[6]

<u>**Source**</u>: **Google.com / (Mizuno Yusho Japan Judo Gi IJF Approved Judogi)**

---

[6] en.wikipedia.org

Source: **Google.com /(Blitz Adult White Diamond 14oz Karate Suit)**

Source: **Google.com/ Jissengata Bogu Set (Kendo Armour)**

Source: Google.com /Japan Kendo Uniform Full Set Armor Iaido Sword Bogu Armour Protection

Sumo

Sumo (相撲) is considered the national sport of Japan, although baseball fans seem to think otherwise. Sumo originated from the Japanese Shinto ritual that depicted a human wrestling a god. Therefore, it is a performance to entertain the Shinto deities.[7]

Sumo is a spiritual sport performed with rituals and traditions. Example: before every match, wrestlers always throw salt on the ring in order to purify it. As for the rules, only men are allowed to practice the sport professionally in Japan. During a competition, the wrestler a **rikishi** (力士) attempts to force his opponent out of a circular and elevated ring, **dohyō** (土俵) made of clay and covered in a layer of san. The wrestler

---

[7] www.japan-guide.com

who first exits the ring or touches the ground with any part of his body besides the soles of his feet loses.

The Japan Sumo Association is the body that manages and controls professional sumo wrestling in Japan, under the jurisdiction of the Japanese Ministry of Education, Culture, Sports, Science and Technology (MEXT).

There are six tournaments held every year: three in Tokyo (January, May and September); one each in Osaka (March), Nagoya (July) and Fukuoka (November) [8]. At the end of each tournament that lasts 15 days during which each wrestler performs in one match per day, the wrestler who wins more matches win the tournament.

There are no weight restrictions or classes in sumo. That means a wrestler sometimes has to fight against someone who is much heavier. As a result, the heavier you are the better it is.

Becoming Ōzeki or Yokozuna

The Japan Sumo Association is the body that promotes a sumo wrestlers to the rank of Ōzeki (大関) or Yokozuna (横綱).

The most desirable title for every sumo wrestler is to become Ōzeki or Yokozuna. However, in order to be promoted ōzeki, a wrestler must have enough power, skill and dignity and grace "**hinkaku**" (品格). He has to achieve a total of at least 33 wins over the three most recent tournaments, including ten or more wins in the tournament just completed. [9]

In order to be elevated to Yokozuna rank, after a tournament, the Yokozuna Deliberation Council, a body appointed by the Japan Sumo

---

[8] http://www.sumo.or.jp

[9] En.wikipedia.org

Association, will provide an independent quality control on Yokozuna promotion.

The council will meet and discuss the performance of the top-ranked wrestlers. The Japan Sumo Association will make a recommendation that a particular Oozeki-ranked wrestler has the necessary attributes to be promoted. Their recommendation is then passed over to the Judging division and then the Board of Directors of the Sumo Association will make the final decision.[10]

Golf in Japanese culture

Japanese love golf. Ever since golf was introduced in Japan more than a century ago it has become part of Japan culture tangled in business culture. The first golf course in Japan is said to have been built on a hilltop in Kobe in 1901 by British businessmen and had only four holes.[11]

Today there are over 2,300 courses and driving ranges for practice can be found almost everywhere.

A few years ago, only registered members could play in golf courses. But now everyone can enjoy playing golf because golf clubs have opened to the public as visitors at a reasonable price.

Baseball in Japan culture

Baseball is called "**yakyū**" (野球) in Japan and it has become the most popular sport in the country. Baseball was introduced to Japan in 1872, by an American called Horace Wilson, who taught English at the Kaisei School in Tokyo. The first baseball team was called the Shimbashi Athletic Club and was established in 1878.[12]

---

[10] En.wikipedia.org

[11] www.golf-in-japan.com

[12] En.wikipedia.org

Professional baseball in Japan began in the 1920s. It was Matsutarō Shōriki, a media owner, who established the Greater Japan Tokyo Baseball Club (大日本東京野球クラブ Dai-Nippon Tōkyō Yakyū Kurabu) a team of all-stars established in 1934. Baseball has been a popular sport ever since.

The Japanese baseball association is called Nippon Professional Baseball and was founded in 1950. But it used to be the Japanese Baseball League **"Nihon Yakyū Renmei"** (日本野球連盟,) which operated from 1936 to 1949.[13]

---

[13] www.asianstudies.org/

CHAPTER 10

PART 1
JAPANESE FAVORITE PASTIME: ARTS

Manga and Anime

Manga (漫画) is the Japanese noun for "comics." It refers to visual stories drawn and told in a way that is unique to the Japanese.

Anime (アニメ) is the transliteration and condensation of the English word "animation." It refers to animated programs created in Japan as well as any animation bearing a distinctively Japanese art and story style.

In the last two decades, the popularity of manga in Japan has grown so much that, today there is a huge domestic an international industry for manga that is still increasing. In Japan, people of both genders and all ages read manga. People read manga everywhere. It is very common to see business men or salary men in suits reading thick comic books in commuter trains.

Manga themes are very diverse. The content ranges from history to futuristic science fiction and from teenage romance to topics dealing with every day's life. Comics target a large audience that can be youth (boys and girls) and adult (male and female). Comics are sold almost everywhere in Japan, including convenience stores, bookstores etc.

It appears that whenever a manga series becomes popular, it is made into an anime. The world-famous animes are "Dragonball", "Sailor Moon", and "Pokemon" and "Cobra". There is a very popular anime production company called "Studio Ghibli" located in Mitaka, near Inokashira Koen, just outside Tokyo. This studio has won numerous award and it attracts visitors from all over the world.

PART 2

MANGA AND ANIME EVENTS

- **manga cafes**

The popularity of manga and anime in Japan has led to the establishment of manga cafes that attract fans of all ages.

Manga cafes are places where people (customers) can go and read from a library of manga for a limited time at a determined fee. Customers can borrow and return books as many times as you wish to, within that limited time. There are manga cafes in all major cities such as Tokyo, Kyoto and Osaka.

- **Maid Cafes**

Maid cafes were created to fulfill the fantasies of fans of maid-themed manga and anime. The concept started in **Akihabara** (秋葉原), Tokyo. Ever since, multiple maid cafes have opened in the area, making Akihabara the best place to go to for a maid cafe experience. The characteristic of maid cafes are the waitresses dressed typically in costumes as French maids. Food and desserts served at the cafes are usually decorated in a cute way. The waitresses play the role of a maid and make customers feel at home.

Example of maid cafes:

- **Maidreamin**

Maidreamin (メイドリーミン) is said to be one of the most popular maid cafes in Japan which has numbers of stores across the country including 7 in Akihabara area.[1]

---

[1] Japan Web Magazine

- **Pinafore**

Pinafore is famous for appearing on the famous TV drama "Densha Otoko" (the Train Man).[2]

- **@home cafe**

@home cafe (@ホームカフェ) is said to be the famous "moe" maid cafe in Japan. Starting from "Welcome home, my master!" you are treated by the extremely cute and moe service. There is also a live show by cute maids who sing and dance.[3]

- **Cure Maid Cafe**

The Cure Maid Café was created in 2001 and offers a Victorian style theme. Cure Maid Cafe serves excellent tea and the cafe is certificated by Japanese Tea Association.[4]

- **The Granvania**

The Granvania is known for serving gourmet food and a huge selection of alcohol beverage including 30 different beers from 12 different countries.[5]

- ● **Events**

There are a few manga and anime grand events held through the year in Japan. For example: the Anime Japan (formerly known as Tokyo Anime Fair) takes place annually at Odaiba's Big Sight convention center, which is one of the largest animation events in the world. The other event is the Comiket, a huge comic book fair which attracts hundreds of thousands of people. It is held biannually, at Big Sight as well, in Tokyo.

---

[2] Japan Web Magazine

[3] Japan Web Magazine

[4] Japan Web Magazine

[5] Japan Web Magazine

PART 3

ANIME INDUSTRY REPORT 2019

The Association of Japanese Animations, is engaged in research, survey, and analysis in connection with the Japanese animation industry. This organization has published.

"Anime Industry Report" since 2009 in order to disseminate information about the industry to the world.

The survey for this report revealed that the market size reached 2 trillion 181.4 billion yen (100.9% of the previous year's), recording the most sales for six consecutive years despite the slight growth.

The overseas market reached 1000 billion yen for the first time, recording 1 trillion 9.2 billion yen (101.4% of the previous year's) while Internet (123.1% of the previous year's) and Live Entertainment (110.2% of the previous year's) showed constant growth.[6]

Tattoo is an "art", is it?

A few years ago, I could see many Japanese people with a tattoo **"irezumi"**(入れ墨) covering part of their arms, legs, and neck. I thought that form of expression was part of Japan culture as it was in the UK or in the US. The drawing was so beautiful that I thought it could only be done by professionals or artists. As time passed by, it appeared that the drawing that I admired watching on some Japanese people's skin, (not on mine because I am afraid of the needle), the Japanese society had a complex relationship with it.

---

[6] The Association of Japanese Animations: Anime Industry Report 2019 (Release date: December 9, 2020)

http://www.spi-information.co

Ever since then, I have come to understand that the yakuza (やくざ) use tattoo as a rite to pledge their allegiance to organized crime they are associated with, with full-body markings. And visitors of Japan are asked to cover up their tattoos when they are in public [7]. Consequently, regardless of their profession they cannot use public swimming pools, hot springs, beaches and even some gyms. A part Japan history shows that there used to be a completely different interpretation of tattoos.

16,000 years ago, in the Jomon era, tattoos were used to identify one's tribe. However, these customs faded away in the Edo era that lasted from 1603 to 1868. [8] During that period, tattoos became a symbol of masculinity and then, as irezumi-kei, the mark of a criminal. The practice ended but the Japanese society and the Government kept a very negative view of tattoos. Exposing a tattooed skin in public was no longer accepted.

The government have since kept pressure on tattoo artists, citing their lack of medical licenses. Which means tattoo artists are now technically committing a crime every time they pick up their tattoo gun, to perform the medical procedure of tattooing. Only medical doctors can legally administer tattoos.[9]

A Health, Labor, and Welfare Ministry notice in 2001 ruled that: "tattooing, along with laser hair removal and chemical peels, is medical work because it involves a needle piercing the skin".[10]

That notice has since been used to prosecute tattoo artists, who claim their work is a form of self-expression and therefore protected under Japan's constitution.

---

[7] Metropolisjapan.com/tattoos-in-japan

[8] Metropolisjapan.com/tattoos-in-japan

[9] CNN. October 19, 2017. Did Japan just ban tattoo artists?

[10] CNN. October 19, 2017. Did Japan just ban tattoo artists?

CHAPTER 11

PART 1

ARTS AND DECORATION - IKEBANA

Ikebana "**arranging flowers**" or "**making flowers alive**" (生け花 or 活け花) is the Japanese art of flower arrangement. It is not only about putting flowers in vase or a mere floral decoration. It is a disciplined art form in which the arrangement is a living thing, where nature and humanity are brought together. It is rooted in the philosophy of developing a closeness with nature.[1]

Ikebana is a creative expression with certain rules of construction. The materials used are living branches, leaves, grasses, and blossoms. The main idea is the beauty resulting from color combinations, natural shapes, graceful lines, and the meaning latent in the total form of the arrangement. Ikebana objective is to bring out the inner qualities of flowers and other live materials and express emotion.

Ikebana in Japanese culture

Buddhists are to thank for the development ikebana in the 6th century. Plants in Shinto tradition were believed to be dwellings for nature spirits used to welcome spirits or deities. From there, Buddhist priests taught people how to elegantly and meaningfully arrange flower offerings for altars. Its popularity spread to nobility and then became a secular activity in the 15th century.[2]

---

[1] http://www.ikebanahq.org/whatis.php

[2] www.tokyocheapo.com/entertainment/Tokyo-ikebana-workshop

Then the pastime of viewing plants and appreciating flowers throughout the four seasons was established in Japan early on through the aristocracy, during the Heian era (794–1185). Ikebana is now taught all over the world. Ikebana's school is often headed by an **iemoto** (家元) translated "family foundation"; often times passed down within a family from one generation to the next.

Source: Photo by Annie Dalbéra, via Wikimedia Commons

An iemoto can also be called O-iemoto, or Sōshō (宗匠) or Ō-sensei (大先生). In English, "Grand Master". His roles are to lead the school and protect its traditions.

Some of the most historic and well-known schools are:

● Ikenobō (池坊) is a development of rikka and considered the oldest school:

- Shōgetsudo Ko-ryū – originated by the monk Myōe (1171–1231)

- Ko-ryū (古流) – originated by Ōun Hoshi or Matsune Ishiro (1333–1402).[3]

PART 2

GARDENING IN JAPAN'S CULTURE

Japanese gardens "**nihon teien**" (日本庭園) make use of natural materials to create scenery and landscapes like one might find in the natural world. They are traditional gardens based on philosophical ideas, designed aesthetically.

The design of Japanese gardens always depends on social climate, geographical features, local weather, and bears the influence of the government of the time in which they were created.

> *For example, during the Heian period (794-1184), when the country was ruled by the Emperor and the nobility in Kyoto, gardens presented the solemn landscapes in line with the ideals of Pure Land Buddhism, such as the garden in front of the* **Phoenix Hall at the Byodo-in temple.**[4]
>
> *In the Muromachi period (1338-1573), the Ashikaga clan established its shogunate government in Kyoto. The clan used the famous Kinkakuji-temple as a villa and had a colorful garden in the perceived Chinese dynastic style created there. The garden's pond contains stones which represent the nine mountains and eight seas said to surround Mt. Meru, believed to be the center of the world in Buddhist thought. Dry stone gardens at Zen temples*

---

[3] en.wikipedia.org/wiki/Ikebana

[4] www.tokyo-park.or.jp/special/botanicallegacy/en/tokyo

*were also created during the Muromachi period, like the **Hojo Garden** at the Ryoan-ji temple in Kyoto.*[5]

*During the Edo period (1603-1867), the capital of Edo was ruled by the Tokugawa samurai clan. Edo contained some 1,000 estates for the various feudal lords from across the country to live in. These lords took the vast grounds given to them by the shogun and built gardens around their mansions – in Japanese, these gardens are called **daimyo teien**, or "**feudal lord gardens**,"* [6].

Source: ja.wikipedia.org/wiki/兼六園 kenrokuen

---

[5] www.tokyo-park.or.jp/special/botanicallegacy/en/tokyo

[6] www.tokyo-park.or.jp/special/botanicallegacy/en/tokyo

Source: en.japantravel.com/kyoto/kyoto-tofuku-ji-s-hojo-garden

Source: google.com/Tokyo Travel: Kiyosumi Teien (Kiyosumi Gardens

The gardens of the feudal lords in Edo were known for having large ponds built in the center of the garden. They were built with paths going around the garden to allow visitors to stroll through.

– In Japanese this type of garden is called **kaiyushiki teien**, or "**circuit-style garden**".[7]

PART 3
SHODŌ (JAPANESE CALLIGRAPHY)

Shodō (書道) also called shūji (習字) is Japanese calligraphy. It is a form of artistic writing of the Japanese language. It is considered to be a skill and aesthetic way of writing. The beauty of shodo is said to come from a combination of techniques accompanied with the flow of the brush and the ink that goes with spiritual concentration.

The term shodō, translated "way of writing" comes from Chinese. It was used to describe the art of Chinese calligraphy during the medieval Tang dynasty and introduced in Japan in the 6th century as a means of communication between the two countries.[8]

SHO (書) means: to write, writing and DO (道) means : the path, the way or the TAO.

The characteristic of Shodō is simplicity, beauty and the connection between the mind and the body.

Tools

The tools also called the "Four Treasures of the Study" of SHODO are the following: the **brush, ink, paper,** and **ink stone.**[9]

Brush "**Fude**" (筆) is said to be the most important tool to best implement the craft. There are two types used, the "**hosofude**" （細筆） which is a slender brush, and the **futofude** (ふと筆), which is a thicker brush usually

---

[7] www.tokyo-park.or.jp/special/botanicallegacy/en/tokyo

[8] www.invaluable.com/blog/japanese-calligraphy

[9] www.invaluable.com/blog/Japanese-calligraphy

made of bamboo with the bristles taken from animals such as the wolf, badger, horse, or squirrel.[10]

Ink "**Sumi**" (墨): made from the soot of pine branches

Mulberry Paper "**Washi**" (和紙): is a traditional Japanese paper tougher than ordinary paper and it absorbs ink better.

Ink stone "**Suzuri**" (硯): used by artists to rub the sumi ink black to create ink.

PART 4

THE RELATIONSHIP BETWEEN SHODO AND ZEN

Japanese calligraphy is said to be an integral element of Zen. It was influenced by Zen thought in the way that for any particular piece of paper, the calligrapher has only one chance to create something with the brush. Which means:

> *The brush strokes cannot be corrected, and even a lack of confidence shows up in the work. The calligrapher must concentrate and be fluid in execution. The brush writes a statement about the calligrapher at a moment in time.[11]*

> *Through Zen, Japanese calligraphy absorbed a distinct Japanese aesthetic often symbolized by the **ensō** or circle of enlightenment.*

Zen calligraphy started with **Wang Xizhi** (303-361), considered to be the most famous Chinese calligrapher and painter. His work is still used today as learning material; many calligraphers copy Xizhi's work on Kaisho

---

[10] www.invaluable.com/blog/Japanese-calligraphy

[11] en.wikipedia.org/wiki/Japanese_calligraphy

(block script) and Sosho (cursive script) as a way to grasp the basics of calligraphy.[12]

Another major influence in Zen Calligraphy is **Kukai** (posthumously known as Kobo Daishi). Kukai was a famous buddhist priest whose cursive style gave birth to the Japanese Hiragana syllabary.[13]

Source: google.com (How to Choose Best Writing Brush for You? - Standards and Types)

Source: google.com Japanese Inkstone Suzuri Sumi Grinder Calligraphy Shodo Tool Shuji...

---

[12] www.gohitsushodostudio.com/shodo-and-zen

[13] www.gohitsushodostudio.com/shodo-and-zen

CHAPTER 12

PART 1
JAPANESE CUISINE

Characteristics

The traditional Japanese cuisine, (和食) translated "Japanese eating", is based on combining the staple food, which is steamed white rice, "**gohan**" (御飯), **okazu** (オカズ), the main dish and a few side dishes. This will always be accompanied with miso soup "**misoshiru**"(みそ汁) and sometimes pickles "**tsukemono**" (漬物) . As for beverage, tea is served preferably.

Rice is served in a small bowl "**chawan**"(茶碗)。 Then the main course is placed on a separate plate "sara"(皿).

Japanese would avoid different-flavored dishes touching each other on a single plate in order to preserve the taste of each individual food. That is the reason different dishes are served separately on own individual plates.

Side dishes often consist of vegetables, grilled seafood or raw, as sashimi or sushi. It can also be deep-fried called **"tempura".** Noodles, such as **"soba"** and **"udon"** are also staple food. There is also another variety of dishes cooked with fish products in broth such as **"oden"**, or beef in **"sukiyaki"** etc…

There is an emphasis on seasonal ingredients. One of the most important characteristics of **Washoku** is said to be seasonality. *Each ingredient is celebrated for its peak season, or **shun** (旬) Respect for nature is a key* aspect of *Shintoism, the main religion in Japan. Washoku is a demonstration of Shinto beliefs.* [1]

Generally, oil is lightly used in Japanese cooking, except for tempura. For that reason, Japanese cuisine has a reputation for being healthy.

History

Japanese cuisine is said to have been influenced by Chinese cuisine before opening up to Western cuisines.[2]

Dishes like **"rāmen" (noodles)** or **"gyōza"**, are from China and food like spaghetti, curry, and hamburgers are rather Western and they are now common on Japanese tables. But in order to suit the Japanese way of eating and taste, all this foreign food had to be modified with local ingredients. Example: *Traditionally, the Japanese shunned meat due to Buddhism, but with the modernization of Japan in the 1880s, meat-based dishes such as **tonkatsu** and **yakiniku** have become common.*[3]

PART 2
IZAKAYA

An **izakaya (居酒屋)** is a Japanese-style pub where a group of people, friends colleagues will gather and enjoy drinking alcohol and have food as well. However, instead of everyone ordering and receiving their own main dish, it is common for everyone to order lots of small and inexpensive dishes that are shared by everyone around the table

---

[1] arigatojapan.co.jp/washoku

[2] en.wikipedia.org/wiki/Japanese cuisine

[3] en.wikipedia.org/wiki/Japanese cuisine

Source: ja.wikipedia.org

Source: ja.wikipedia.org

PART 3

IMPORTANT EXPRESSIONS

"Itadakimasu!" (頂きます) has no real equivalent in English. It can be translated as"*I humbly take*". It is away to thank the host for preparing the meal. But you also have to thank everyone involved in the process, starting from the farmers tilling the fields, to the plants and animals that were sacrificed to become the meal.

"Gochisousama!" (ごちそうさま) is literally translated *"It has been a feast,"* this is said at the end of the meal to acknowledge respectfully that the host has worked hard to prepare for your meal.[4]

Kampai! (Cheers!)

In Japanese culture, drinking plays an important role. Drinking parties, typically held at restaurants and izakaya, are a common activity that are used to strengthen both social and business ties. A large variety of alcoholic beverages can be found in Japan. Some of the most popular ones are:

Beer

Beer is the most popular alcoholic drink in Japan. Due to taxation issues, several types of beer-like beverages have emerged in recent years, including happoshu and new-genre of beer. These beverages are taxed less because they contain less or no malt, and can be sold at lower prices.[5]

Sake (Rice Wine)

Sake or **nihonshu** (日本酒) ("sake" is also the general Japanese term for alcohol) is brewed using rice, water and **koji mold** as the main ingredients. There are countless local rice wines **"jizake"**(地酒). The alcohol rate of nihonshu is typically about 10-20 percent. It can be drunk either hot or cold.[6]

---

[4] arigatojapan.co.jp/washoku

[5] www.japan-guide.com

[6] www.japan-guide.com

Chūhai

Chūhai （酎ハイ） (shortened from "shochu highball") are fruit-flavored alcoholic drinks with alcohol rate between 3~8 percent. Common flavors include lemon, **ume**, peach, grapefruit and lime in addition to seasonal flavors. Chuhai are made of shochu and soda, and are available premixed in cans anywhere alcohol is sold.[7]

Wine

Wine is gaining popularity in Japan, especially among women. While imported red, white, and sparkling wines from France, Italy, the United States, Chile and Australia are widely available. There is also an increasing domestic wine industry. The most famous wine producing region in Japan is the Kofu basin in Yamanashi Prefecture.[8]

PART 4
EATING AND DRINKING OUT

Japanese people regularly eat and drink out, which is called "**gaishoku**" (外食). That is the reason restaurants and Izakaya are always crowed. However, it is important to know that pouring you own glass in Japan is considered not polite.

It is customary in western countries to serve others before you serve yourself. But in Japan you are never supposed to pour yourself a drink. If you have poured for others, another guest will certainly notice that your glass is empty and will fill it before drinking.

---

[7] www.japan-guide.com

[8] www.japan-guide.com

Tipping

In Japanese culture, tipping is considered rude, and can even be seen as degrading. Tipping will often cause confusion, and many people will chase after you to give you back your money.

If someone has been particularly helpful and you feel absolutely compelled to leave a tip, leaving a small present instead would be preferable.

ja.wikipedia.org/wiki/寿司 Sushi

<u>Source:</u> Japanese-tradition.com (a typical Japanese meal set)

SUSHI displayed at SEIYU. Help yourself please!

CHAPTER 13

PART 1
JAPANESE MUSIC

In Japan, you can listen to any genre of music (音楽). Local media, TV channels and various radio stations broadcast all day long both traditional and modern music.

Japan is said to be the largest physical music market in the world, worth US$2 billion in sales in physical formats in 2014, and the second-largest overall music market, worth a total retail value of 2.6 billion dollars in 2014 [1]

Local music often appears at karaoke venues, which is on lease from the record labels.

Enka

Enka (演歌) is a popular Japanese music genre considered to resemble traditional Japanese music stylistically. It is characterized by *slow ballads in vibrato* style.

Vibrato is when a singer sings a note at a fluctuating pitch. The effect is a bit echo-like. The type of vibrato that Enka singers employ is called **"kobushi"** (こぶし) and it is a slightly different style of vibrato that employed by opera singers, as the pitch only fluctuates to one degree.

---

[1] The International Federation of the Phonographic Industry Releases Its 2014 Data on the World Music Market" aramajapan.com

Generally, Enka performers usually dress in traditional Japanese kimono when they perform, that is the reason why Enka is perceived as if it is a very ancient form of Japanese singing.[2] Enka is said to be rather a cultural pop music phenomenon developed during the 20th century. Enka most popular singer is **Kitajima Saburou.**[3]

PART 2
HOUGAKU AND GAGAKU

Hougaku, (邦楽) is defined as traditional Japanese music meaning music from Japan or home music. It is opposed to Western music "**yougaku**" (洋楽).[4]

Gagaku (雅楽,)"elegant music"or "imperial court music" is the oldest form of traditional or classical music in Japan. It includes songs, dances, and a mixture of other Asian music. It was established in the court around 1, 200 years ago. It has been preserved ever since at the Imperial court and in some shrines and temples.[5]

PART 3
TYPICAL JAPANESE MUSICAL INSTRUMENTS

Koto

The **Koto,** (箏) also called kin, is a long Japanese board zither having 13 silk strings and movable bridges. The body of the instrument is made of *paulownia wood* and is about 190 cm (74 inches) long.

---

[2] www.definitions.net/definition/ENKA

[3] www.musicgenreslist.com/music-enka/

[4] https://japanesetradmusic.blogspot.com/p

[5] http://iha-gagaku.com/english/gagaku.html (TRADITIONAL MUSIC OF JAPAN)

When the performer is kneeling or seated on the floor, the Koto is held off the floor by two legs or a bridge-storage box; in most modern concerts, the instrument is placed on a stand so the performer can sit on a chair.

The Koto is played by plucking the strings with the thumb and first two fingers of the right hand, which are fitted with ivory plectrums called **tsume**. The left hand, in traditions after the 16th century, may alter the pitch or sound of each string by pressing or manipulating the strings to the left of the bridges.[6]

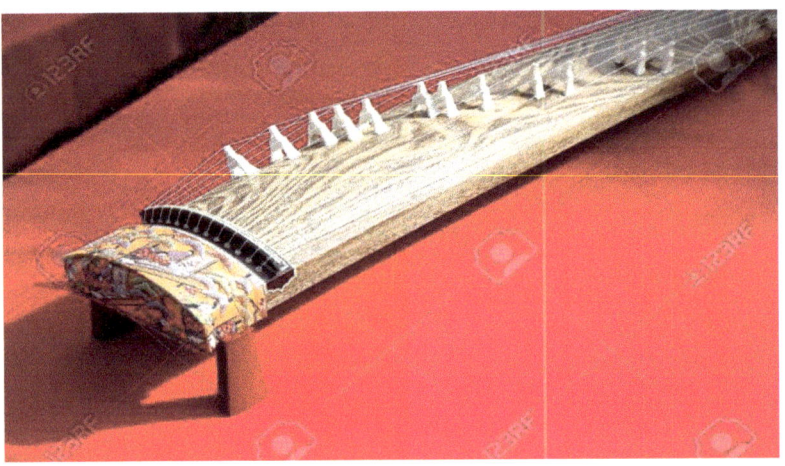

Source: google.com (Traditional Japanese instrument, the Koto)

Biwa

The **biwa** (琵琶) is a Japanese short-necked fretted lute, distinguished by its graceful, pear-shaped body The biwa has a shallow, rounded back and silk strings (usually four or five) attached to slender lateral pegs. The instrument is played with a large wedge-shaped plectrum called a **Bachi.** The strings are tuned in fourths, and the melody is played almost exclusively on the highest pitched string.[7]

---

[6] www.britannica.com/art/koto

[7] www.britannica.com/art/biwa

In Japanese Buddhism, the biwa is the chosen instrument of **Benten** (弁天), goddess of music, eloquence, poetry, and education. The biwa was first popular in China and then spread throughout East Asia. It is said to have arrived in Japan from China during the Nara period (710 - 794).[8]

Source: google.com (Traditional Japanese biwa)

Wadaiko(和太鼓) **Japanese style Drum**

Source: google.com (Japanese Taiko)

---

[8] en.wikipedia.org/wiki/Biwa

Ryuuteki

The **Ryuuteki**, (竜笛) is a Japanese transverse flute also known as "dragon flute" made of bamboo. It is often used in **gagaku.**

Source: Google.com (Plastic Japanese Ryuteki Flute- Gagaku Instrument)

Shamisen

The **shamisen**, (三味線) is a three-stringed Japanese instrument similar to a **banjo**. It originated from China and was introduced to Japan in the 16th century.[9]

---

[9] Google.com (traditional Japanese instrument)

<u>Source</u>: Google.com (Traditional NEW WOOD Monstera Red Sanshin Shamisen Okinawa Ryukyu

CHAPTER 14

PART 1

THE GOVERNMENT OF JAPAN

The Government of Japan "**Nipponseifu**" (日本政府) is a constitutional monarchy in which the power of the Emperor is limited. The Government runs under the framework established by the Constitution of Japan, adopted in 1947, and it is divided into three branches: the Legislative, the Executive, and the Judicial branch.[1]

The legislative branch.

The legislative branch "**Rippoufu**" (立法府), also known as the National Diet "**kokkai**" （国会）is bicameral, consisting of two houses: The upper house or House of Councilors) "**san in**" (参院) and the Lower house or House of representatives "**shuugi in**" (衆議院).

> *The House of Representatives is composed of 480 members, of whom 300 are elected from the single-seat constituencies and 180 by the proportional representation system in which the nation is divided into 11 electoral blocs which according to size return between 6 and 30 members. Their term of office is 4 years, but shall be terminated, before the full term is up, if the House is dissolved.*

- Japan.kantei.go.jp/ constitution_and_government_of_japan/

> *The total membership of the House of Councilors is 242, of whom 96 are elected by the proportional representation system from a*

---

[1] en.wikipedia.org/wiki/Government_of_Japan /

single nationwide electoral district and 146 from 47 prefectural constituencies, each returning 2 to 8 members. Their term of office is 6 years, and a half of the members being elected every 3 years.[2]

The executive branch

The Executive branch of Japan "**gyousei kikan**" (行政機関)is headed by the Prime Minister. The Prime Minister, "**Naikakusōri daijin**" (内閣総理大臣) who must be a civilian, is the head of the Cabinet. He is designated by the legislative organ, the National Diet, and appointed by the Emperor.[3]

The Cabinet, which is the source of power, consists of the Ministers of State. They may be appointed or dismissed by the Prime Minister. If the Cabinet loses confidence and support to be in office by the Diet with a motion of no confidence, the Cabinet has to resign en masse or when the post of Prime Minister becomes vacant. Unless the House of Representatives is dissolved within ten days.[4]

Judicial branch

The Judicial branch "**Shihou-fu**" (司法府) consists of the Supreme Court, four other lower courts; the High Courts, District Courts, Family Courts and Summary Courts.

The Chief Justice is appointed by the Emperor, but the other Justices of the Supreme Court are appointed by the Cabinet. The Judges of inferior

---

[2] http://japan.kantei.go.jp/constitution_and_government_of_japan

[3] http://japan.kantei.go.jp/constitution_and_government_of_japan

[4] http://japan.kantei.go.jp/constitution_and_government_of_japan

courts are also appointed by the Cabinet but only from a list of people nominated by the Supreme Court.[5]

PART 2: THE EMPEROR OF JAPAN

The Emperor of Japan **"ten noo"** (天皇) is the head of the Imperial Family. He is defined by the Constitution to be "*the symbol of the State and of the unity of the people*".[6] The Imperial Throne is dynastic and succeeds from father to son.

The Emperor is not the nominal Chief Executive and he has no real power related to the Government as stated clearly in article 4 of the Constitution. He possesses only certain ceremonially important powers, such as:

- *The appointment of the Prime Minister as designated by the Diet.*

- *The appointment of the Chief Justice of the Supreme Court as designated by the Cabinet.*

- *The promulgation of amendments of the constitution, laws, cabinet orders and treaties.*

- *The convocation of the Diet.*

- *The dissolution of the House of Representatives.*

- *The proclamation of general election of members of the Diet.*

- *The attestation of the appointment and dismissal of Ministers of State and other officials as provided for by law, and of full powers and credentials of Ambassadors and Ministers.*

- *The attestation of general and special amnesty, commutation of punishment, reprieve, and restoration of rights.*

---

[5] http://japan.kantei.go.jp/constitution_and_government_of_japan

[6] Article 1, Section 1 of the Constitution of Japan (1947)

- *Awarding of honors.*

- *The attestation of instruments of ratification and other diplomatic documents as provided for by law.*

- *Receiving foreign ambassadors and ministers.*

- *The performance of ceremonial functions.* [7]

---

[7] http://japan.kantei.go.jp/constitution_and_government_of_japan/

CHAPTER 15

PART 1
ERAS IN JAPAN

In Japanese culture, there is a system of era names called "**nengō**" (年号= year name) or "**gengō**" (元号) used to count years. The current era is "**REIWA**" (令和), which began when Emperor Naruhito succeeded his father Akihito on April 30, 2019, when the latest abdicated the throne.

Two elements are to consider in order to express years in Japan: the first is "gengo" and the second is the number that indicates the year within the era, followed by "nen" (年). Example: "REIWA NI NEN"(令和 2 年), which means "REIWA YEAR TWO".

Gengō

In Japan, emperors are posthumously named after their eras. For example, the former emperor's father, whose name was Emperor Hirohito during his reign, is now called Emperor Shōwa, as emperors are never called by their personal names even during their reign. Instead, the emperor is always referred to as "Tennō Heika" (天皇陛下), meaning: His Majesty the Emperor or "Kinjō Tennō" (今上天皇), meaning: the current emperor.

Gregorian calendar years and equivalent nengō year since 1868

1868　明治　Meiji　or Myōji=> Emperor Meiji, 1868–1912.

1912　大正　Taishō　=> Emperor Taishō, 1912–1926.

1926　昭和　Shōwa　=> Emperor Shōwa, 1926–1989.

1989　平成　Heisei　or Byōsei => Emperor Akihito, 1989–2019.

2019　令和　Reiwa　or Ryōwa => Emperor Naruhito, 2019–present.

<u>Source</u>: en.wikipedia.org/

PART 2
ABBREVIATIONS

Era names can be abbreviated by taking the first letter of their Romanized names. As follow: T40 means Taishō 40; S55 means Shōwa 55; and H22 for Heisei 22. Shōwa is the longest era to date, at 62 years and 2 weeks.

REIWA

The current era is Reiwa (令和), interpreted as *"beautiful harmony"*,[1] began on the 1st of May, 2019, following the 31st and final year of the Heisei era "HEISEI SANJU ICHI NEN" (平成 31 年 = Heisei year 31). While the Heisei era (平成) started on the 8th of January 1989), after the death of Emperor Hirohito.

The Reiwa era (令和) began the day after Emperor Akihito voluntarily abdicated [2]. Emperor Akihito, rather than serving in his role until his death, as it is the rule, received a special one-time permission for his abdication. His elder son, Naruhito, ascended to the throne as the 126th Emperor of Japan on the 1st of May 2019.

PART 3
HISTORICAL NENGŌ

Era names originated in 140 BCE in China, during the reign of the Emperor Wu of Han [3]. However, the system of the imperial era is said to

---

[1] "Government says Reiwa translates as 'beautiful harmony'". The Asahi Shimbun. April 3, 2019.

[2] NHK："天皇陛下 「生前退位」 の意向示される ("His Majesty The Emperor Indicates His Intention to 'Abdicate'")" (in Japanese). 13 July 2016.

[3] En.wikipedia.org:

have been established in the year 645 during the reform of Taika under the reign of Emperor Kotoku. The first imperial era recorded in Japan is therefore called the Taika era and lasted until the year 650 of the Gregorian calendar. Ever since, 247 gengō was recorded, and the current is the 248th recorded on the 1st of April 2019.

Since the Japanese constitution was adopted in 1947, it is the Government that decides the name of the era:

- The Prime Minister chooses a panel of renowned scholars. These scholars are requested to come up with potential names that would be appropriate for the new era. Every scholar has to propose several gengo with two kanji.

- The name chosen must have a proper meaning reflecting the nation ideals and ambition, and must also have a positive meaning. The kanji chosen should be easy to read and easy write by every Japanese.[4]

Source: ja.wikipedia.org/wiki/元号 Gengou (Keizo Obuchi, then chief cabinet secretary, announcing the Heisei era in 1989, when Emperor Akihito ascended to the throne)

---

[4] japan-experience.com

Source: ja.wikipedia.org/wiki/元号 Gengou (April 1st, 2019 at 11.30 am, Chief Cabinet Secretary Yoshihide Suga announced Reiwa as the name of the new era in Japanese history)

CHAPTER 16

PART 1
STYLE - FASHION

Fashion in Japan changes very fast, and is well known through the world. It appears that, to see the trend in fashion in Japan, to need to spend a few hours in a day on the streets of, Ikebukuro, Akihabara, Ginza, Odaiba, Shinjuku, Nakameguro, Aoyama, Shibuya and Harajuku, because these areas of Tokyo are famous for their lively street fashion culture. These places give you an overview of how the stylish are driving the Japanese Fashion industry. In a blink of an eye, you will be able to spot new styles for girls, boys, women and men clothing, bags, shoes and accessories from the streets to the stores that sell those items.

In Harajuku, you will certain encounter colorful Gyaru fashion (ギャル) or Lolita fashion.

Gyaru fashion

Gyaru describes women who follow a type of Japanese street fashion which originated in the 1970s. It is a fashion that rejects the Japanese standards of its society. It highlights the refusal of women who are expected to be housewives, with pale skin and dark hair.

Gyaru fashion is characterized by having heavily bleached or dyed hair, tanned skin, highly elongated, decorated nails, and dramatic makeup that consists of dark eyeliner, fake eyelashes, using colored contacts to change the color of their eyes and make the eyes appear larger.

Lolita fashion

Lolita fashion (ロリータ・ファッション) is a subculture from Japan that is highly influenced by Victorian clothing and styles from the Rococo period.

Lolita fashion is supposed to be aesthetic and cute. The clothing theme can be Gothic, Classic, Sweet, Sailor, Country, Hime (princess), Ero (erotic), Guro (grotesque), Oriental, Punk, Shiro (white) and Kuro (black) etc.[1]

Source: www.google.com STUDIO ALTA SHINJUKU: GYARU YOUNG WOMEN'S DEPARTMENT STORE, SHOPP

---

[1] En.wikipedia.org (Gallery)

Source: google.com (Harajuku's Lolita Fashion - Savvy Tokyo)

PART 2

JAPANESE CLOTHING AND WESTERN CLOTHING

Japanese wear traditional clothing known as **wafuku** (和服), as well as Western clothing known as **yōfuku** (洋服).The most well-known form of traditional Japanese fashion is the kimono（着物）meaning "something to wear" Western clothing and fashion are popular in Japan mostly because they are abundant and cheap unlike Japanese traditional clothing that are increasingly expensive and difficult to wear. As a matter of fact, it has become rare to see people wear traditional clothing as everyday clothes.

Traditional garments are now mainly worn for ceremonies or special events, such as summer festivals where the yukata is suitable, or graduation ceremonies to mark the moment. Geisha, Maiko and sumo wrestlers are the group of people who regularly wear traditional clothing because their profession requires it.

Kimono

The kimono (着物) is labelled as the national costume of Japan.[2] Kimono vary in construction, and they are worn by men and women but they are completely different in terms of accessories worn with them. The type of fabric and decoration style for women is also different from men's.

The kimono is commonly worn wrapped around the body, left side over right, and it is sometimes worn layered. The kimono is always worn with an ***Obi***, and may be worn with traditional **Yukata.**

Yukata (浴衣) is an informal kimono worn specifically in the spring and summer. The fabric the yukata is made of is light weight cotton and it is for warm weather. It is basically worn when getting out a bath at home or at a hot sprint for example and it can also be worn as pajamas. However, men and women can be seen wearing Yukata during fireworks or festival events. Yukata is less expensive than the traditional kimono.

Kimono Accessories

● Obi (帯) is a kind of belt or sash for a kimono. There are many kinds and patterns. Women's obis are wider and men's are much narrower and simpler in design.

---

[2] Assmann, Stephanie. "Between Tradition and Innovation: The Reinvention of the Kimono in Japanese Consumer Culture.

<u>Source</u>: ja.wikipedia.org/wiki/帯 Obi (women style) (kimono)

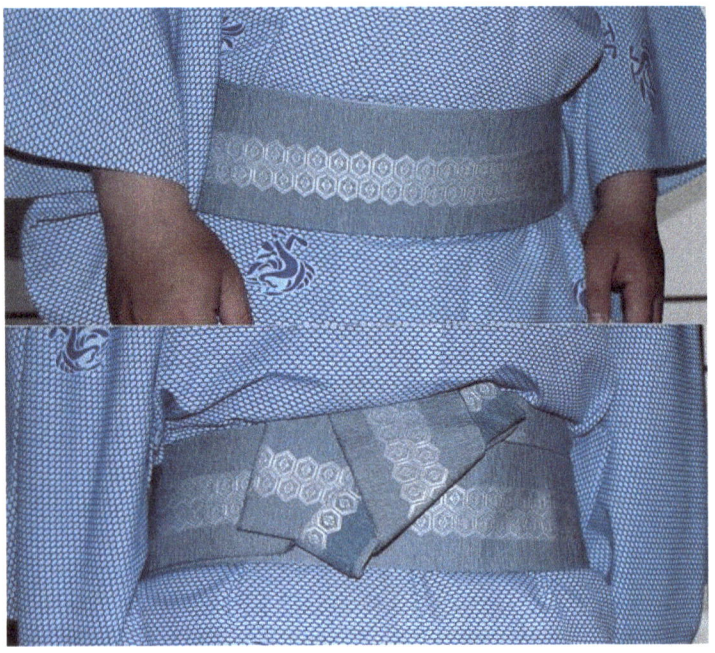

<u>Source</u>:ja.wikipedia.org/wiki/帯 Obi (men Style)

Source: Google.com (Introduction to Types of Obis for women - Kaede Kimon)

Source: Google.com (How to tighten men's obi / In AKimono)

● Nagajuban (長襦袢) is a long undergarment for ladies and men which is worn under the kimono.

Source: Google.com (Two Piece Undergarment Kimono NagaJuban for women)

Source: Google.com (KYOETSU Men's Japanese Kimono Summer underwaear Nagajuban)

- **Kanzashi** （簪）are ornate hairpins used for ladies' traditional hairstyles.

<u>Source</u>: Google.com (Sakura Tsumami Kanzashi Fan Hairpin)

- Hakama (袴) are a kind of long pleated skirt worn by men or women over a kimono. Men wear hakama to formal occasions, while women might wear hakama if they take part in martial arts such as kyūdo, or kendo, or for university graduation ceremonies [3]

---

[3] En.wikipedia.org

Source: Google.com (Ladies Hakama Style)

Source: google.com (KYOETSU Men's Japanese Striped Hakama)

- **Haori** (羽織) is a jacket worn over kimono by men and women.

Source: Google.com (Burgundy silk haori/kimono jacket/Japanese vintage kimono for women)

Source: Google.com (Japanese silk Haori blue men flawless jacket)

- **Tabi** (足袋) are split-toed socks worn with **zōri** or **geta** sandals.

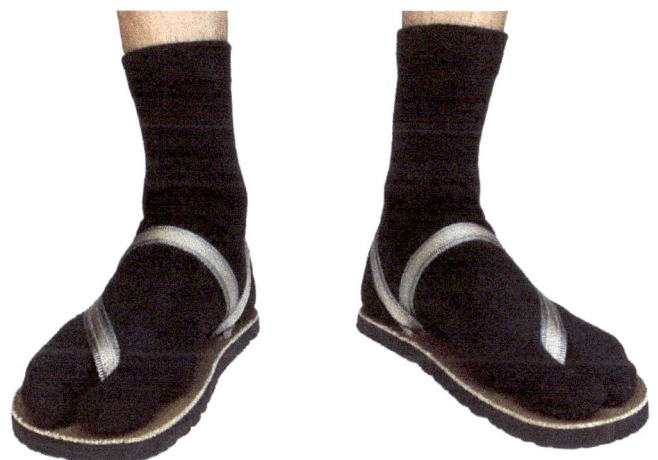

Source: Google.com (Crew Wool Tabi Socks - Black / Earth Runners)

- **Zōri** (草履) are thonged sandals often made with leather, cloth, or vinyl, and which should be worn with tabi socks.

Source: Google.com (Zori sandals)

● **Geta** (下駄) are wooden sandals which can be worn with or without **tabi** socks.

Source: Google.com (Geta Sandals - Kiri /Black)

CHAPTER 17

PART 1
JAPAN ECONOMY I （日本経済）

Japan is the third-largest economy in the world by nominal Gross Domestic Product (GDP), right behind the USA and China, respectively first and second. Its workforce is large and well-educated. With the population of 126.5 million, Japan has the fourth largest consumer markets in the world [1].The standard of living in Japan is very high, with the GDP/capita estimated around USD 40,000.[2]

Japan is one of the world leaders in the manufacture of electrical appliances and electronics, automobiles, ships, machine tools, optical and precision equipment, machinery and chemicals. However, China and the Republic of Korea have gained great economic advantage in manufacturing those same products.

The World Bank defines a high-income economy as a country with a gross national income per capita of US$12,536 or more in 2019, calculated using the Atlas method.[3] Therefore, Japan is viewed as a high-income country.

---

[1] Asialinkbusiness.com.au

[2] Asialinkbusiness.com.au

[3] World Bank (World Bank Country and Lending Groups) Accessed on September 9, 2020

PART 2

JAPAN AS A MEMBER OF APEC, WTO, CPTPP, G-20 AND G7

- APEC

Japan is a member of Asia-Pacific Economic Cooperation, which is an economic group of 21 members, formed in 1989. Its main objective is to promote free trade and sustainable development in the Pacific Rim economies.

The birth of APEC was a response to the proliferation of regional economic blocs, such as the European Union (EU) and the North American Free Trade Area (NAFTA), although is dead now.[4]

- WTO

Japan is part of the World Trade Organization which is the successor to the GATT (General Agreement on Tariffs and Trade).

And the original GATT text (GATT 1947) is still in effect under the WTO framework, subject to the modifications of GATT 1994.[5]

- CPTPP

Since July 6, 2018 Japan has become part of the CPTPP (Comprehensive and Progressive Agreement for Trans-Pacific Partnership), which includes: Australia, Brunei, Canada, Chile, Malaysia, Mexico, New Zealand, Peru, Singapore and Vietnam.[6]

The CPTPP was signed on March 8th, 2018, in Santiago, Chile. The objective and the benefits are that nearly 98% of the customs duties be

---

[4] investopedia.com

[5] investopedia.com

[6] Pacific Customs Brokers Ltd

removed at the time of final implementation. Once CPTPP comes into force, many commodities would be duty free upon entry. The elimination of tariffs will depend on the staging category. Some items will have the duty reduced faster than others. A few commodities will not be reduced at all.

Following the United States' withdrawal from the TPP in January 2017, Japan drove the process forward to salvage the deal. Among the objectives of the CPTPP are to:

- Realize expeditiously the benefits of the TPP and their strategic and economic significance;

- Contribute to maintaining open markets, increasing world trade and creating new economic opportunities for people of all incomes and economic backgrounds;

- Promote further regional economic integration and cooperation between the parties; and

- Promote high standards on human rights, labor practices and the environment.[7]

- G.20

The G20 was formally established in September 1999 and brings together finance ministers and central bank governors from 19 countries: Argentina, Australia, Brazil, Canada, China, France, Germany, India, Indonesia, Italy, Japan, the Republic of Korea, Mexico, Russia, Saudi Arabia, South Africa, Turkey, the United Kingdom, the United States of America plus the European Union, which is represented by the President of the European Council and by Head of the European Central Bank.

Objectives of the G20:

---

[7] NEWZEALAND FOREIGN AFFAIRS & TRADE

- Coordinate policies between its members in order to achieve global economic stability and sustainable growth.

- Promote financial regulations that reduce risks and prevent future financial crises in other words strengthen the international financial system;

- Reform and modernize international financial institutions.[8]

- G7

Source: www.thesun.co.uk

The G7 or the Group of Seven, are seven of the largest economies of the world. The group was founded in the early 1970s as the seven countries

---

[8] www.g20.org

discussed concerns about the collapse of the oil industry. The members are: Canada, France, Germany,Italy, Japan, the United Kingdom and the United States. Together, they represent more than 62 per cent of the global net wealth ($280trillion).[9]

The group was previously known as the G8 and counted Russia among its members, but Russia has been excluded since annexing the Crimean Peninsula from Ukraine in early 2014.

Summits are held annually, and hosted on a rotation basis by the group's members. It offers the leaders of these nations the chance to come together and tackle the most challenging global issues of the time, such as "security policy", "climate change" and "disarmament programs".[10]

PART 3
JAPAN ECONOMY II - EXPORT AND IMPORT

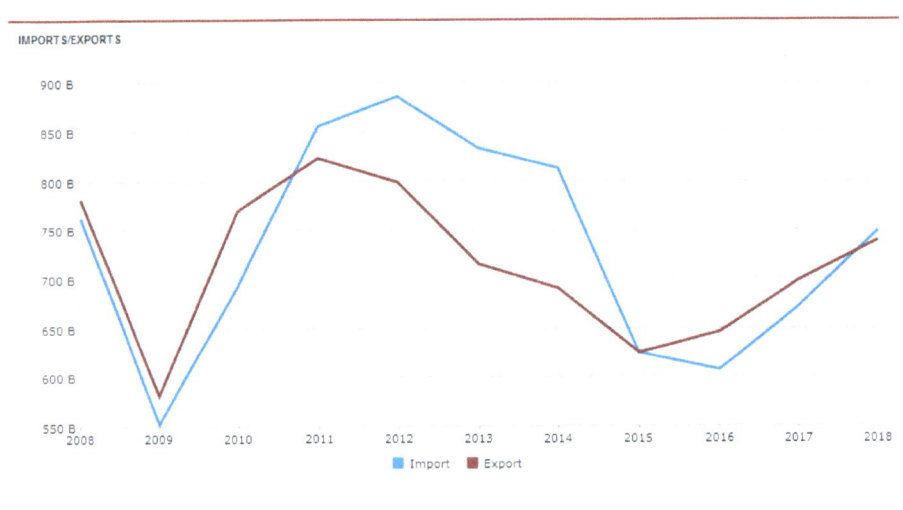

Source: www.wits.worldbank.org (Japan Trade summary: WITS DATA)

---

[9] www.thesun.co.uk

[10] www.thesun.co.uk

Japan Country Growth v/s World Growth v/s GDP Growth

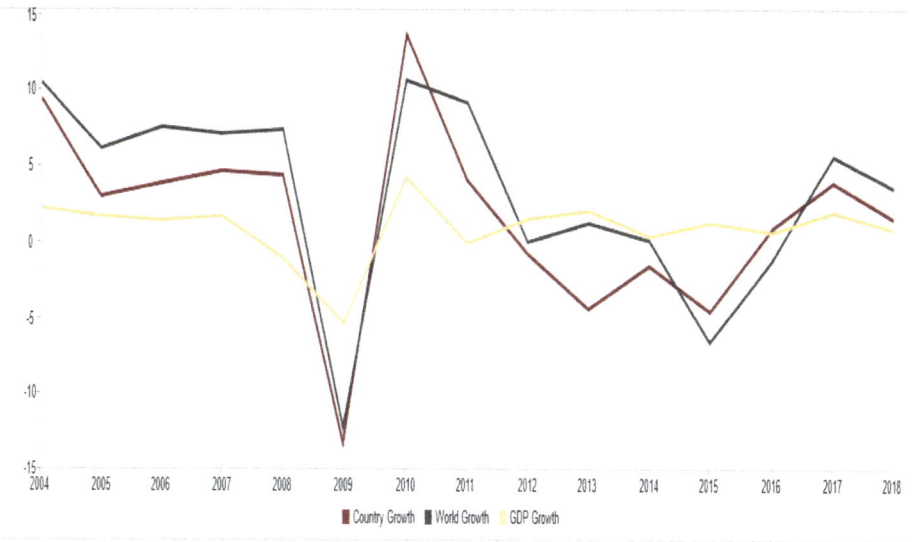

Source: www.worldbank.org (WITS: World Integrated Trade Solution

In 2018, Japan had a total export of 738,201,192.21 in thousands of US$ and total imports of 748,217,608.15 in thousands of US$ leading to a negative trade balance of -10,016,415.94 in thousands of US$.

The trade growth is 1.50% compared to a world growth of 3.50%. GDP of Japan is 4,971,323,079,800 in current US$.

Japan services export is 193,670,505,270 in Bop, current US$ and services import is 200,914,438,210 in Bop, in current US$. Japan exports of goods and services as percentage of GDP is 18.45% and imports of goods and services as percentage of GDP is 18.19%.

Market	Trade (US$ Mil)	Partner share (%)
China	144,053	19.51
United States	140,664	19.05
Korea, Rep.	52,482	7.11
Other Asia, nes	42,394	5.74

Market	Trade (US$ Mil)	Partner share (%)
Hong Kong, China	34,723	4.70

Exporter	Trade (US$ Mil)	Partner share (%)
China	173,612	23.20
United States	83,571	11.17
Australia	45,680	6.11
Saudi Arabia	33,775	4.51
Korea, Rep.	32,112	4.29

Source: www.worldbank.org

PART 4
JAPAN'S MAIN EXPORTS. - SEP 30, 2020

- Vehicles: US$148.8 billion (21.1% of total exports)
- Machinery including computers: **$137 billion** (19.4%)
- Electrical machinery, equipment: **$103.1 billion** (14.6%)
- Optical, technical, medical apparatus: $39.1 billion (5.5%)
- Iron, steel: $26.1 billion (3.7%)
- Plastics, plastic articles: $25.2 billion (3.6%)

Japan's major imports. - Jun 10, 2020

- Mineral fuels including oil: US$155.6 billion (21.6% of total imports)
- Electrical machinery, equipment: $98.8 billion (13.7%)
- Machinery including computers: $70.5 billion (9.8%)

- Optical, technical, medical apparatus: **$28.2 billion** (3.9%)

- Pharmaceuticals: **$27.2 billion** (3.8%)

- Vehicles: **$23.8 billion** (3.3%)

Source: www.worldbank.org

Japan 2018 Trade Flow: Export

Partner Name	No Of exported HS6 digit Products	Export Share in Total Products (%)	Export (US$ Thousand)	Export Partner Share (%)
World	4,219	100.00	738,201,192.21	100.00
East Asia & Pacific	4,118	97.61	368,624,906.72	49.94
North America	3,205	75.97	149,998,005.10	20.32
China	3,555	84.26	144,053,344.74	19.51
United States	3,175	75.25	140,663,642.06	19.05
Europe & Central Asia	3,282	77.79	100,136,576.55	13.56
Korea, Rep.	3,294	78.08	52,482,082.15	7.11
Other Asia, nes	3,317	78.62	42,393,797.65	5.74
Hong Kong, China	3,051	72.32	34,723,305.69	4.70
Thailand	3,094	73.33	32,274,586.00	4.37
Latin America & Caribbean	2,201	52.17	29,929,517.74	4.05

Partner Name	No Of exported HS6 digit Products	Export Share in Total Products (%)	Export (US$ Thousand)	Export Partner Share (%)
Middle East & North Africa	2,225	52.74	24,254,920.82	3.29
Singapore	2,595	61.51	23,410,984.57	3.17
Germany	2,228	52.81	20,891,820.70	2.83
Australia	2,024	47.97	17,088,153.51	2.31
Vietnam	2,946	69.83	16,435,073.61	2.23
South Asia	2,494	59.11	16,073,756.67	2.18
Indonesia	2,639	62.55	15,792,848.21	2.14
Malaysia	2,488	58.97	13,941,421.20	1.89
United Kingdom	2,067	48.99	13,900,852.17	1.88
Netherlands	1,759	41.69	12,716,902.37	1.72
Mexico	1,655	39.23	11,624,698.90	1.57
Philippines	2,487	58.95	11,273,127.65	1.53
India	2,194	52.00	11,011,075.40	1.49
Canada	1,752	41.53	9,326,062.19	1.26
United Arab Emirates	1,550	36.74	7,897,390.60	1.07
France	1,996	47.31	7,323,266.97	0.99

Partner Name	No Of exported HS6 digit Products	Export Share in Total Products (%)	Export (US$ Thousand)	Export Partner Share (%)
Russian Federation	1,522	36.07	7,297,373.19	0.99
Belgium	1,400	33.18	6,817,902.12	0.92
Sub-Saharan Africa	1,502	35.60	6,549,667.00	0.89
Panama	535	12.68	5,921,366.16	0.80
Italy	1,885	44.68	4,701,102.20	0.64
Saudi Arabia	1,174	27.83	4,113,845.12	0.56
Brazil	1,458	34.56	3,999,944.81	0.54
Switzerland	1,234	29.25	3,773,786.69	0.51
Spain	1,461	34.63	3,403,732.94	0.46
Turkey	1,282	30.39	3,190,945.21	0.43
New Zealand	1,224	29.01	2,613,481.26	0.35
South Africa	1,106	26.21	2,519,316.22	0.34
Israel	951	22.54	2,162,767.16	0.29
Poland	1,092	25.88	2,135,755.50	0.29
Pakistan	1,100	26.07	2,097,819.84	0.28
Oman	499	11.83	2,029,132.97	0.27
Chile	799	18.94	1,994,620.49	0.27

Partner Name	No Of exported HS6 digit Products	Export Share in Total Products (%)	Export (US$ Thousand)	Export Partner Share (%)
Kuwait	749	17.75	1,780,667.12	0.24
Hungary	810	19.20	1,645,540.98	0.22
Czech Republic	930	22.04	1,634,393.77	0.22
Bangladesh	1,178	27.92	1,567,876.29	0.21
Sweden	944	22.38	1,431,800.52	0.19
Qatar	690	16.35	1,421,780.67	0.19
Marshall Islands	231	5.48	1,340,491.44	0.18
Austria	835	19.79	1,320,485.92	0.18
Sri Lanka	1,017	24.11	1,251,033.41	0.17
Bahamas, The	193	4.57	1,197,871.64	0.16
Liberia	242	5.74	1,156,857.02	0.16
Colombia	637	15.10	1,110,087.92	0.15
Ireland	553	13.11	1,076,188.67	0.15
Egypt, Arab Rep.	795	18.84	994,636.17	0.13
Norway	578	13.70	930,263.30	0.13
Kenya	410	9.72	897,796.77	0.12
Argentina	837	19.84	738,925.74	0.10

Partner Name	No Of exported HS6 digit Products	Export Share in Total Products (%)	Export (US$ Thousand)	Export Partner Share (%)
Peru	639	15.15	736,202.29	0.10
Iran, Islamic Rep.	633	15.00	697,190.87	0.09
Myanmar	1,194	28.30	693,405.86	0.09
Malta	309	7.32	676,197.56	0.09
Bahrain	518	12.28	643,849.34	0.09
Luxembourg	236	5.59	613,404.46	0.08
Macao	697	16.52	609,623.32	0.08
Portugal	752	17.82	583,526.16	0.08
Uzbekistan	308	7.30	526,288.84	0.07
Mongolia	635	15.05	517,786.76	0.07
Denmark	759	17.99	505,512.94	0.07
Finland	744	17.63	491,361.39	0.07
Romania	552	13.08	444,239.32	0.06
Ecuador	407	9.65	429,264.52	0.06
Jordan	473	11.21	426,721.71	0.06
Cambodia	1,082	25.65	422,272.96	0.06
Greece	547	12.97	420,946.06	0.06

Partner Name	No Of exported HS6 digit Products	Export Share in Total Products (%)	Export (US$ Thousand)	Export Partner Share (%)
Ukraine	441	10.45	418,423.25	0.06
Kazakhstan	299	7.09	387,611.14	0.05
Iraq	376	8.91	359,591.72	0.05
Nigeria	403	9.55	328,157.89	0.04
Tanzania	246	5.83	318,863.62	0.04
Lebanon	427	10.12	315,299.21	0.04
Costa Rica	349	8.27	278,164.96	0.04
Dominican Republic	301	7.13	259,676.22	0.04
Guam	358	8.49	258,249.20	0.04
Georgia	182	4.31	254,466.66	0.03
Jamaica	153	3.63	246,271.97	0.03
Guatemala	288	6.83	230,242.93	0.03
Slovak Republic	313	7.42	223,034.48	0.03
Uganda	269	6.38	199,768.77	0.03
Morocco	418	9.91	195,071.04	0.03
Yemen	172	4.08	188,916.07	0.03
Estonia	320	7.58	164,025.28	0.02

Partner Name	No Of exported HS6 digit Products	Export Share in Total Products (%)	Export (US$ Thousand)	Export Partner Share (%)
Cyprus	253	6.00	161,599.43	0.02
Ghana	345	8.18	151,602.99	0.02
Trinidad and Tobago	277	6.57	148,591.98	0.02
Papua New Guinea	341	8.08	147,980.70	0.02
Bulgaria	377	8.94	146,337.27	0.02
Bolivia	257	6.09	143,587.30	0.02
Mauritius	292	6.92	139,360.85	0.02
Tunisia	260	6.16	138,470.05	0.02
Lao PDR	523	12.40	133,180.25	0.02
Gibraltar	60	1.42	132,893.90	0.02
El Salvador	300	7.11	130,653.31	0.02
Slovenia	390	9.24	127,612.61	0.02
Algeria	276	6.54	125,673.91	0.02
Mozambique	187	4.43	123,715.42	0.02
Paraguay	289	6.85	105,042.97	0.01
Brunei	294	6.97	99,330.76	0.01
Fiji	216	5.12	96,081.39	0.01

Partner Name	No Of exported HS6 digit Products	Export Share in Total Products (%)	Export (US$ Thousand)	Export Partner Share (%)
Honduras	227	5.38	94,267.27	0.01
Iceland	118	2.80	85,668.10	0.01
Cote d'Ivoire	179	4.24	77,702.40	0.01
Lithuania	400	9.48	70,399.30	0.01
Suriname	90	2.13	67,551.00	0.01
Haiti	115	2.73	66,538.55	0.01
Latvia	257	6.09	66,356.64	0.01
Uruguay	296	7.02	63,965.67	0.01
Senegal	152	3.60	61,278.28	0.01
Afghanistan	176	4.17	59,446.47	0.01
Zambia	147	3.48	58,235.84	0.01
Congo, Dem. Rep.	205	4.86	57,045.83	0.01
Nicaragua	145	3.44	56,988.88	0.01
Cayman Islands	73	1.73	56,590.81	0.01
Azerbaijan	128	3.03	55,365.65	0.01
Nepal	289	6.85	52,580.28	0.01
Guyana	90	2.13	50,707.13	0.01

Partner Name	No Of exported HS6 digit Products	Export Share in Total Products (%)	Export (US$ Thousand)	Export Partner Share (%)
Ethiopia(excludes Eritrea)	191	4.53	46,832.74	0.01
Croatia	160	3.79	45,520.50	0.01
New Caledonia	152	3.60	40,356.71	0.01
Sudan	165	3.91	39,580.19	0.01
Cuba	201	4.76	38,791.31	0.01
Djibouti	132	3.13	34,942.97	0.00
Barbados	100	2.37	32,127.99	0.00
Libya	127	3.01	32,038.77	0.00
Northern Mariana Islands	176	4.17	31,801.73	0.00
Togo	101	2.39	31,230.65	0.00
Malawi	107	2.54	29,448.30	0.00
Belarus	161	3.82	29,417.08	0.00
Zimbabwe	117	2.77	29,321.25	0.00
Botswana	57	1.35	28,860.00	0.00
Gabon	96	2.28	26,539.79	0.00
Curacao	111	2.63	25,606.26	0.00
Maldives	189	4.48	25,085.61	0.00

Partner Name	No Of exported HS6 digit Products	Export Share in Total Products (%)	Export (US$ Thousand)	Export Partner Share (%)
Armenia	79	1.87	24,725.51	0.00
Serbia, FR(Serbia/Montenegro)	151	3.58	24,065.35	0.00
Namibia	84	1.99	23,289.28	0.00
Unspecified	61	1.45	21,340.51	0.00
Syrian Arab Republic	133	3.15	20,737.81	0.00
Belize	36	0.85	20,412.56	0.00
French Polynesia	131	3.11	20,412.41	0.00
Tuvalu	29	0.69	20,179.07	0.00
Angola	146	3.46	19,927.37	0.00
Cameroon	122	2.89	19,918.00	0.00
Venezuela	140	3.32	19,753.23	0.00
Micronesia, Fed. Sts.	213	5.05	19,297.44	0.00
Burkina Faso	45	1.07	18,164.12	0.00
Antigua and Barbuda	43	1.02	17,695.56	0.00
Guinea	72	1.71	17,687.50	0.00
Turkmenistan	145	3.44	17,496.47	0.00

Partner Name	No Of exported HS6 digit Products	Export Share in Total Products (%)	Export (US$ Thousand)	Export Partner Share (%)
Eswatini	45	1.07	17,379.99	0.00
Solomon Islands	149	3.53	17,044.71	0.00
Mauritania	43	1.02	16,702.62	0.00
Kyrgyz Republic	148	3.51	16,585.29	0.00
Madagascar	131	3.11	15,707.34	0.00
Mali	41	0.97	15,387.93	0.00
Palau	294	6.97	15,083.05	0.00
Samoa	116	2.75	13,669.66	0.00
Tonga	114	2.70	13,624.05	0.00
St. Lucia	51	1.21	12,722.82	0.00
Tajikistan	75	1.78	12,593.03	0.00
Rwanda	57	1.35	11,228.00	0.00
Seychelles	65	1.54	10,971.03	0.00
Vanuatu	68	1.61	10,951.71	0.00
Lesotho	50	1.19	10,792.06	0.00
Montenegro	52	1.23	10,193.43	0.00
Benin	47	1.11	9,443.88	0.00

Partner Name	No Of exported HS6 digit Products	Export Share in Total Products (%)	Export (US$ Thousand)	Export Partner Share (%)
Grenada	34	0.81	9,163.07	0.00
Bhutan	81	1.92	8,839.35	0.00
Cape Verde	41	0.97	8,560.17	0.00
Bermuda	61	1.45	8,300.85	0.00
St. Vincent and the Grenadines	75	1.78	7,782.38	0.00
Dominica	55	1.30	7,457.66	0.00
Burundi	26	0.62	7,295.71	0.00
Sierra Leone	37	0.88	7,231.78	0.00
East Timor	117	2.77	7,181.19	0.00
British Virgin Islands	28	0.66	6,790.66	0.00
North Macedonia	57	1.35	6,582.47	0.00
Moldova	64	1.52	6,525.15	0.00
St. Kitts and Nevis	30	0.71	6,425.11	0.00
Congo, Rep.	54	1.28	6,413.74	0.00
Kiribati	102	2.42	6,236.31	0.00
Somalia	33	0.78	6,180.51	0.00

Partner Name	No Of exported HS6 digit Products	Export Share in Total Products (%)	Export (US$ Thousand)	Export Partner Share (%)
South Sudan	62	1.47	5,532.48	0.00
Turks and Caicos Isl.	20	0.47	5,362.62	0.00
Niger	19	0.45	5,164.10	0.00
Gambia, The	18	0.43	5,094.77	0.00
Cook Islands	26	0.62	3,088.44	0.00
Chad	17	0.40	2,989.80	0.00
Anguilla	22	0.52	2,859.79	0.00
Bosnia and Herzegovina	25	0.59	2,733.31	0.00
Occ.Pal.Terr	29	0.69	2,692.82	0.00
Niue	10	0.24	2,500.77	0.00
American Samoa	16	0.38	2,257.48	0.00
Comoros	15	0.36	2,204.11	0.00
Nauru	27	0.64	1,998.77	0.00
Central African Republic	64	1.52	1,909.20	0.00
Albania	36	0.85	1,447.66	0.00
Eritrea	5	0.12	979.94	0.00
Sao Tome and Principe	3	0.07	867.76	0.00

Partner Name	No Of exported HS6 digit Products	Export Share in Total Products (%)	Export (US$ Thousand)	Export Partner Share (%)
Equatorial Guinea	28	0.66	585.03	0.00
Andorra	10	0.24	396.84	0.00
Montserrat	9	0.21	363.45	0.00
Tokelau	1	0.02	142.42	0.00
Guinea-Bissau	7	0.17	124.16	0.00
Saint Helena	7	0.17	93.14	0.00
Western Sahara	11	0.26	54.01	0.00
Falkland Island	5	0.12	38.85	0.00
Greenland	1	0.02	2.26	0.00

Source: www.worldbank.org

CHAPTER 18

PART 1
MILITARY

Article 9 of the Japanese Constitution

1.   Aspiring sincerely to an international peace based on justice and order, the Japanese people forever renounce war as a sovereign right of the nation and the threat or use of force as means of settling international disputes.

2.   In order to accomplish the aim of the preceding paragraph, land, sea, and air forces, as well as another war potential, will never be maintained. The right of belligerency of the state will not be recognized.[1]

The Jeitai Foundation

As stated in Article 9 of the Japanese Constitution, Japan isn't legally allowed to have a military, but Japan does have a military. It is called The Japan Self-Defense Forces (自衛隊, Jie Itai; abbreviated JSDF), also known as the Self-Defense Forces (SDF).

The JSDF, controlled by the Ministry of Defense, was founded by the Self-Defense Forces Law in 1954 and the Prime Minister is the commander-in-chief.

---

[1]   https://www.loc.gov/law/help/japan-constitution/article9.php (Library of Congress Law)

Like any country in the world, Japan has a ground force (the largest); a marine and an air force.

Japan-Self Defense Forces flag (JSDF)

Source : mod.go.jp

PART 2

JAPAN GROUND SELF-DEFENSE.

The Japan Ground Self-Defense Force (陸上自衛隊, Rikujō Jieitai), JGSDF, also known as the Japanese Army, was created on July 1, 1954. It is the land warfare branch of the Japan Self-Defense Forces. Its head quarter is located in Ichigaya and Shinjuku in Tokyo. The JGSDF counted about 150,000 soldiers in 2018.

Source: https://en.wikipedia.org (Emblem of the Japan Ground Self-Defense Force)

Japanese Ground Self Defense Forces: Artillery

Source: www.crwflags.com

Japan Maritime Self-Defense Force

Source: www.crwflags.com (Japan Maritime Self-Defense Flag)

The Japan Maritime Self-Defense Force (Japanese: 海上自衛隊, Kaijō Jieitai, abbreviated JMSDF), also known as the Japanese Navy, is the maritime warfare branch of the Japan Self-Defense Forces.

The JMSDF was formed following the dissolution of the Imperial Japanese Navy (IJN) after World War II. [2] The JMSDF has a fleet of 154 ships and 346 aircraft and consists of approximately 45,800 personnel. Its

---

[2] Library of Congress Country Studies: (Japan National Security Self-Defense Forces)

main tasks are to maintain control of the nation's sea lanes and to patrol territorial waters. It also participates in UN-led peacekeeping operations (PKOs) and Maritime Interdiction Operations (MIOs).

Japan Air Self-Defense Force

Source: https://commons.wikimedia.org (Flag of the Japan Air Self-Defense Force)

The Japan Air Self-Defense Force (航空自衛隊, Kōkū Jieitai), JASDF, also referred to as the Japanese Air Force, is the air warfare branch of the Japan Self-Defense Forces. It is responsible for the defense of Japanese airspace and aerospace operations. JASDF was established on July 1, 1954 when the Defense Agency replaced the Security Agency, in order to bear the defense mission of Japan of the Ground Self-Defense Force.

The JASDF carries out combat air patrols around Japan, while also maintaining a network of ground and air early-warning radar systems. The branch also has an aerobatic team known as Blue Impulse and has provided air transport in UN peacekeeping missions.[3]

---

[3] Library of Congress Country Studies (http://lcweb2.loc.gov/frd/cs)

The JASDF had an estimated over 50,000 personnel, including 46,942 airmen and 2,971 civilian officials in 2018,[4] and about 740 aircraft, approximately 330 of them fighter aircraft in 2020.[5]

---

[4] www.mod.go.jp/asdf/English_page/organization/formation

[5] Flightglobal.com (World Air Forces Machine)

CHAPTER 19

PART 1
JAPAN TRANSPORTATION SYSTEM

Japanese public transportation is characterized by its punctuality despite the large crowds of people using it. The service is superb and effective, particularly within metropolitan areas and large cities. Travelling from one part of the country to another is easy and convenient for anyone who wants to discover the beauty of this magnificent country.

However, when it comes to travelling, it will always depend on how far, how comfortable and fast you wish to travel. You may choose to travel by plane, train (Shinkansen or regular trains), buses, metro or subway or cabs.

PART 2
TRAVELLING WITHIN A CITY

Getting around within any city in Japan is very convenient. You can choose to ride the bus, the metro or get a cab.

- The Metro or subway

Japan's large cities, such as Tokyo, Osaka, Kyoto, Nagoya and Kobe are served by a great subway train and metro networks that is operated by Japan Railways abbreviated JR, and various private companies.

Trains start to operate as early as 5 am and end around midnight. And trains come and go every five minutes or so.

- City buses

City buses are an alternative to the train, metro or subway to get around many cities in Japan.

In Tokyo, Kyoto, Osaka, Nagoya, and other touristic spots, there are special city buses that follow a tourist sightseeing route. These buses are always scheduled to stop at the most famous attraction sights in the city to allow visitors to get off and buy souvenir products.

Tokyo: Odakyu Bus

● Cabs

Cabs or taxi stands are usually located outside train stations and other landmarks in any Japanese city. However, for foreigners who cannot communicate in Japanese, it would be preferable to have your destination written down on a piece of paper or marked on a map then relay that information to the cab driver. It would facilitate your journey.

Tokyo Taxi

PART 3

LONG-DISTANCE TRAVEL

- **Plane**

There are several airline companies that offer domestic travel in Japan. But the big two that operate the majority of the flights in almost every part of the country are Japan Airlines (JAL) and All Nippon Airways (ANA).

- The JAL Group consists of JAL Domestic and JAL International, as well as of several smaller airlines including Japan Transocean Air, Ryukyu Air Commuter and others. The JAL Group serves over 50 airports and over 100 domestic routes in Japan.[1]

---

[1] www.japan-guide.com

The ANA Group consists of All Nippon Airways, as well as several smaller airlines such as Air Nippon. The ANA Group serves about 50 airports and 100 domestic routes in Japan.[2]

Source: www.jal.co.jp/en/787

Source: www.ana.co.jp/share/wallpaper/image/ B767-300 Takamatsu

---

[2] www.japan-guide.com

There are also a number of smaller and cheaper rates airlines that compete with JAL and ANA, such as: Skymark Airlines, Peach Aviation, Jetstar Japan, Spring Airlines Japan, Air Do, Solaseed Air, Fuji Dream Airlines, IBEX Airlines, etc...[3]

Shinkansen

Most of Japan's major cities are connected by a high-speed bullet train network that is run by the Japan Railways Group (JR Group). Known as the Shinkansen （新幹線）, these bullet trains can travel up to speeds of 320 kilometers per hour.

Source : www.japan-guide.com

---

[3] www.japan-guide.com

PART 4

WHAT IS SUICA OR PASMO?

Suica is a prepaid IC card issued by JR East for JR trains in the Greater Tokyo, Niigata and Sendai regions.

Pasmo is also a prepaid IC card used to travel on Tokyo's railway, subway and bus operators other than JR.

IC cards such as Suica, Pasmo, Icoca, Pitapa, Manaca, Kitaca etc… are rechargeable cards that can be used to conveniently pay fares on public transportation and to make payments at vending machines, shops and restaurants by simply touching the card on a reader for about one second.

How to use your IC card?

When passing through an automatic ticket gate, touch the card onto the card reader for about one second rather than inserting it into the ticket slot. The applicable fare will be automatically deducted when you exit through the ticket gate at your destination station. When riding buses, card readers are placed at the entrance and/or exit of the bus.

How to recharge your IC card?

IC cards can be recharged at ticket machines and special re-charging machines found at railway stations and other locations into down.

How to check your IC card balance?

The current credit balance of your IC card is always shown on a small display whenever you pass through a ticket gate or make a payment at a store. The balance can also be checked at ticket machines.

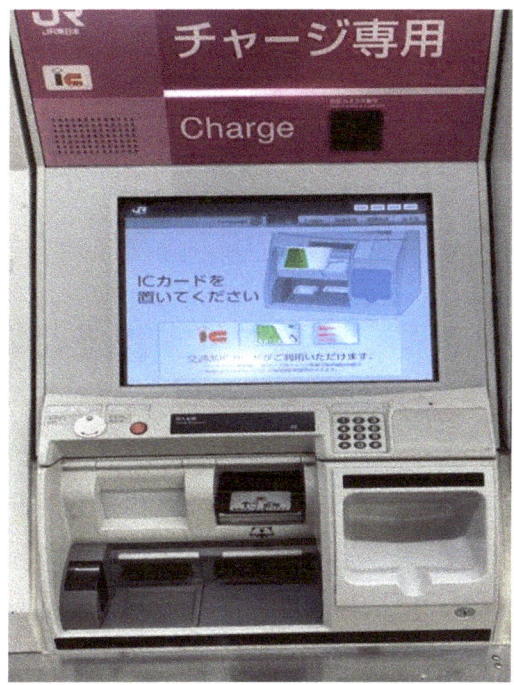

Recharge only

Ticket machine with recharge option

<u>Source</u> : www.pasmo.co.j

BIBLIOGRAPHY

Assmann, S. (2008). "*Between Tradition and Innovation: The Reinvention of the Kimono in Japanese Consumer Culture.*" Fashion Theory: The Journal of Dress, Body & Culture 12

Bernal, H. & Kathryn A. *(2007). Kamikaze Girls and Loli-Goths. Fashion in Fiction Conference.* University of Technology, Sydney, *Australia.*

Bernal, H. & Kathryn A. (2011). The Lolita Complex: A Japanese fashion subculture and its paradoxes (Thesis). Auckland University of Technology. p. 20.

Chanoyu A. (2007) V*ocabulary: Practical Terms for the Way of Tea* (Kyoto: Tankosha,) "Iemoto" entry by Francis L. K. Hsu in Kodansha Encyclopedia of Japan "いけばな流派大集合".

Dreager, Donn F. (1974). *Modern Bujutsu & Budo - The Martial Arts and Ways of Japan.* New York/Tokyo: Weatherhill. p. 11.

Fitts, R. (2016) "*Vintage Japanese Baseball Cards,*" Baseball History http://tinyurl.com/zm6tkz2.

Gall J. & Engel, G. (2006) *Sayonara Home Run! The Art of the Japanese Baseball Card* (San Francisco: Chronicle Books).

Gatlin, Chancy *J. (2014). The Fashion of Frill: The Art of Impression Management in the Atlanta Lolita and Japanese Street Fashion Community (Thesis). Georgia State University.*

Haijima*, A. (2013). Japanese Popular Culture in Latvia: Lolita and Mori Fashion (Thesis).* University of Latvia.

Hall, David A. (2012) *Encyclopedia of Japanese Martial Arts.* Kodansha USA.

Karl F. (1997). *Legacies of the Sword. Hawai*: University of Hawai'i Press. p. 63.

King, D. (1991) *"A History of Japanese Baseball Cards,"* Japanese Baseball Card Quarterly.

Kubota, Jun (2007). *Iwanami Nihon Koten Bungaku Jiten* (in Japanese). Iwanami Shoten. Nihon Koten Bungaku Daijiten: Kan'yakuban [A Comprehensive Dictionary of Classical Japanese Literature: Concise Edition]. Tōkyō: Iwanami Shoten.

Spacey, J. (2015). "*16 Traditional Japanese Fashions*". Japan Talk.

Pocorobba, J. & Kikuoka H. (2003) Metropolis "*Japanese Classical Music*", Weekend Edition Sunday, August 24,

Ratti O. & Westbrook, A. (1991). *Secrets of the Samurai: The Martial Arts of Feudal Japan*. Tuttle Publishing.

Shirahata Y. (2016) *DAIMYO GARDENS* Translated by Imoto C. and Lynne E. Riggs English translation © 2016 International Research Center for Japanese Studies, Kyoto Printed by Dohosha Printing Co.

Vovin, A. (2008).*"Proto-Japanese Beyong Accent System"* In *Frellesvig, Bjarne*

Whitman, J. (2008) *(Eds.). Proto-Japanese: Issues and Prospects. Current Issues in Linguistic Theory. John Benjamins. pp. 141– 156*

www.ingramcontent.com/pod-product-compliance
Ingram Content Group UK Ltd.
Pitfield, Milton Keynes, MK11 3LW, UK
UKHW021417220425

5564UKWH00037B/536